# Company's Coming®

# Cookies

Jean Paré

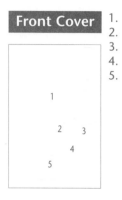

1. Shortbread Pinwheels, page 64
2. Orange Bran Cookies, page 12
3. Gum Drops, page 44
4. Peanut Butter Cookies, page 139
5. Chocolate Softies, page 49

**Cookies**
Copyright © Company's Coming Publishing Limited

Published by
Company's Coming U.S.A., L.C. © 2005
Maitland, Florida, USA 32751
Tel: 407-916-1950
Fax: 407-916-0600

Printed in The United States of America

# Collect the Series

*"I collect many cookbooks but these are the best I've found."*
Louise R. - Pennsylvania, U.S.A.

*"Thanks for making our family's eating experience so tasty and enjoyable!"*
Myra W. - Tennessee, U.S.A.

To order
see back
pages

*"When I want to prepare something different, these are the cookbooks I reach for."*
Donna Z. - Iowa, U.S.A.

*continued on next page*

# Collect the Series

*"Thank you for making the best set of cookbooks there is!"*
Joyce F. - New York, U.S.A.

 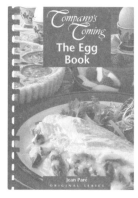 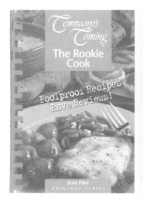

*"I have given a few of your cookbooks as gifts. My friends enjoy them very much."*
Ann Louise B. - Pennsylvania, U.S.A.

*Quick & easy recipes, everyday ingredients!*

To order see back pages

*"The directions are so clear and so perfect it is impossible to mess up!"*
Carol S. - New York, U.S.A.

# Table of Contents

# The Company's Coming Story

Jean Paré (pronounced "jeen PAIR-ee") grew up understanding that the combination of family, friends and home cooking is the best recipe for a good life. From her mother, she learned to appreciate good cooking, while her father praised even her earliest attempts in the kitchen. When Jean left home, she took with her a love of cooking, many family recipes and an intriguing desire to read cookbooks as if they were novels!

*"never share a recipe you wouldn't use yourself"*

In 1963, when her four children had all reached school age, Jean volunteered to cater the 50th Anniversary of the Vermilion School of Agriculture, now Lakeland College, in Alberta, Canada. Working out of her home, Jean prepared a dinner for more than 1,000 people, which launched a flourishing catering operation that continued for over 18 years. During that time, she had countless opportunities to test new ideas with immediate feedback—resulting in empty plates and contented customers! Whether preparing cocktail sandwiches for a house party or serving a hot meal for 1,500 people, Jean Paré earned a reputation for good food, courteous service and reasonable prices.

As requests for her recipes mounted, Jean was often asked the question, "Why don't you write a cookbook?" Jean responded by teaming up with her son, Grant Lovig, in the fall of 1980 to form Company's Coming Publishing Limited. The publication of *150 Delicious Squares* on April 14, 1981 marked the debut of what would soon become one of the world's most popular cookbook series.

The company has grown since those early days when Jean worked from a spare bedroom in her home. Today, she continues to write recipes while working closely with the staff of the Recipe Factory, as the Company's Coming test kitchen is affectionately known. There she fills the role of mentor, assisting with the development of recipes people most want to use for everyday cooking and easy entertaining. Every Company's Coming recipe is *kitchen-tested* before it's approved for publication.

Jean's daughter, Gail Lovig, is responsible for marketing and distribution, leading a team that includes sales personnel located in major cities across Canada. In addition, Company's Coming cookbooks are published and

distributed under license in the United States, Australia and other world markets. Bestsellers many times over in English, Company's Coming cookbooks have also been published in French and Spanish.

Familiar and trusted in home kitchens around the world, Company's Coming cookbooks are offered in a variety of formats. Highly regarded as kitchen workbooks, the softcover Original Series, with its lay-flat plastic comb binding, is still a favorite among readers.

Jean Paré's approach to cooking has always called for *quick and easy recipes* using *everyday ingredients.* That view has served her well. The recipient of many awards, including the Queen Elizabeth Golden Jubilee medal, Jean was appointed a Member of the Order of Canada, her country's highest lifetime achievement honor.

Jean continues to gain new supporters by adhering to what she calls The Golden Rule of Cooking: *"Never share a recipe you wouldn't use yourself."* It's an approach that works—*millions of times over!*

# Foreword

Visions of all kinds are conjured up at the very mention of the word "cookies." Opening the door upon arriving home from school to the heavenly aroma of freshly baked cookies leaves an indelible print in one's mind. Baking a batch of cookies will bring back enthusiasm to youngsters who are "dying of boredom."

Of course there are memories of sneaking a few forbidden cookies as well as taking "just one" from the freezer day after day until somehow the freezer carton is nearly empty. Some deeds can't be covered up.

This book contains many varieties. Ice box cookies that are made one day and baked the next are always enjoyed. Drop cookies such as Hermits and Chocolate Nuggets are great for lunch and snacks. Fancy tea rolls such as Brandy Snaps make a fussy "tea" complete.

Every cookie in this book is pictured in full color. Browse through at your leisure and choose an assortment of shapes and sizes for baking. Planning ahead? Every cookie can be frozen.

Baking time varies due to the thickness and size of each cookie. Overbaking causes dryness and hardness. Room must be left for expansion. If baking sheets have sides, turn upside down and use bottoms. This makes

cookies easier to remove from the pan. When using two baking sheets in your oven at the same time, exchange the top sheet with the bottom sheet and reverse both from front to back half way through baking.

When company's coming—any age or any size of crowd—be ready for the onslaught with a full cookie jar.

*Jean Paré*

# Florentines

*An elegant cookie! Bottoms are spread with chocolate.*
*Contain almonds and peel.*

| | |
|---|---|
| Butter (or hard margarine) | 1/4 cup |
| Granulated sugar | 1/2 cup |
| Whipping cream | 1/4 cup |
| All-purpose flour | 2 tbsp. |
| Flaked almonds | 1 cup |
| Candied orange peel, finely chopped | 1/2 cup |
| Chopped candied cherries | 2 tbsp. |
| Semisweet chocolate chips | 1/2 cup |

In small saucepan combine butter, sugar and cream. Heat, stirring until it boils. Remove from heat.

Stir in flour, almonds, orange peel and cherries. Drop 2 measuring tsp. per cookie onto greased baking sheet. Spread with spoon. Bake in 350°F oven for 10 to 12 minutes. With pancake lifter, push in edges a bit all around to make a good neat edge. Let stand until you are able to remove them without tearing, about 3 or 4 minutes. Cool.

Melt chips in heavy saucepan over low heat. Spread flat side (bottom) of cookies with chocolate. Let stand 1/2 hour. Crease in wavy lines with fork. Makes 2 dozen.

Pictured on page 143.

---

### Paré Pointer
*Naturally you would expect homeless dogs to be in an arf-anage.*

# Pumpkin Cookies

*A spicy drop that is economical as well as popular.*

| | |
|---|---|
| Butter (or hard margarine), softened | 1/2 cup |
| Brown sugar, packed | 1 1/4 cups |
| Large eggs | 2 |
| Vanilla | 1 tsp. |
| Canned pumpkin (or fresh cooked and mashed) | 1 cup |
| All-purpose flour | 2 cups |
| Baking powder | 4 tsp. |
| Salt | 1/2 tsp. |
| Cinnamon | 1/2 tsp. |
| Nutmeg | 1/2 tsp. |
| Cloves | 1/4 tsp. |
| Ginger | 1/4 tsp. |
| Raisins or chocolate chips | 1 cup |
| Chopped nuts | 1 cup |

Cream butter and sugar together well. Beat in eggs 1 at a time. Add vanilla and pumpkin.

Stir remaining ingredients together and add. Mix well. Drop by tablespoonfuls onto greased pan. Bake in 375°F oven for about 15 minutes until lightly browned. Makes 5 1/2 dozen.

Pictured on page 71.

# Orange Coconut Cookies

*The flavor of coconut comes through well in these.*

| | |
|---|---|
| Butter (or hard margarine), softened | 1 cup |
| Grated orange rind | 2 tbsp. |
| Granulated sugar | 1 1/4 cups |
| Large eggs | 2 |
| Milk | 1/4 cup |
| All-purpose flour | 2 cups |
| Baking powder | 2 1/4 tsp. |

*(continued on next page)*

Drop Cookies

| Cinnamon | 3/4 tsp. |
|---|---|
| Salt | 1/4 tsp. |
| Rolled oats | 1 cup |
| Shredded coconut | 3/4 cup |

Cream butter, orange rind and sugar together well. Beat in eggs 1 at a time. Add milk.

Stir flour, baking powder, cinnamon and salt together and add to butter mixture. Mix together.

Stir in oats and coconut. Drop by spoonfuls onto greased baking sheet. Bake in 400°F oven for 8 to 10 minutes. Makes 4 dozen.

Pictured on page 71.

# Cornflake Cookies

*Resembles a butter cookie with spice added.*

| Butter (or hard margarine), softened | 1/2 cup |
|---|---|
| Granulated sugar | 1/2 cup |
| Brown sugar, packed | 1/2 cup |
| Large egg | 1 |
| Vanilla | 1/2 tsp. |
| All-purpose flour | 1 cup |
| Baking powder | 1 tsp. |
| Salt | 1/4 tsp. |
| Cinnamon | 1/2 tsp. |
| Ginger | 1/4 tsp. |
| Nutmeg | 1/4 tsp. |
| Cloves | 1/8 tsp. |
| Cornflakes | 1 1/2 cups |
| Chopped dates or raisins (optional) | 1 cup |

Cream butter and both sugars together. Beat in egg and vanilla.

Add remaining ingredients. Mix well. Drop by spoonfuls onto greased baking sheet. Bake in 350°F oven for 10 to 12 minutes. Makes 2 1/2 to 3 dozen.

Pictured on page 71.

Drop Cookies

# Orange Bran Cookies

*A wonderful breakfast cookie.*

| | |
|---|---|
| Butter (or hard margarine), softened | 1/2 cup |
| Granulated sugar | 1/2 cup |
| Large egg | 1 |
| Prepared orange juice | 2 tbsp. |
| Grated orange rind | 1 1/2 tsp. |
| All-purpose flour | 1 cup |
| Baking powder | 1 tsp. |
| Salt | 1/2 tsp. |
| Bran flakes cereal | 1 cup |
| Semisweet chocolate chips (optional) | 1 cup |

Cream butter and sugar together. Beat in egg. Add orange juice and rind.

Add remaining ingredients. Mix well. Drop by spoonfuls onto greased cookie sheet. Bake in 350°F oven for 10 to 12 minutes. Makes 3 dozen.

Pictured on cover.

# Peanut Molasses Cookies

*A different flavor combination.*

| | |
|---|---|
| Butter (or hard margarine), softened | 1/2 cup |
| Granulated sugar | 1/2 cup |
| Large egg | 1 |
| Smooth peanut butter | 3/4 cup |
| Table molasses | 1/2 cup |
| All-purpose flour | 1 1/4 cups |
| Rolled oats | 1 cup |
| Baking powder | 2 tsp. |
| Baking soda | 1/4 tsp. |
| Salt | 1/2 tsp. |

Cream butter and sugar together well. Beat in egg. Mix in peanut butter and molasses.

Stir remaining ingredients together and add. Mix well. Drop by spoonfuls onto ungreased baking sheet. Flatten with floured glass or with fork. Bake in 375°F oven for 12 to 15 minutes. Makes about 3 dozen.

Pictured on page 71.

# Butterscotch Oat Drops

*The addition of butterscotch chips makes these doubly good.*

| | |
|---|---|
| Butter (or hard margarine), softened | 1 cup |
| Granulated sugar | 1/2 cup |
| Brown sugar, packed | 1 cup |
| Large eggs | 2 |
| Vanilla | 1 tsp. |
| All-purpose flour | 2 cups |
| Rolled oats | 2 cups |
| Baking soda | 1 tsp. |
| Baking powder | 1 tsp. |
| Salt | 1 tsp. |
| Butterscotch chips | 2 cups |
| Chopped nuts (optional) | 1 cup |

Combine butter and both sugars in bowl. Cream well. Beat in eggs 1 at a time. Add vanilla.

Measure in remaining ingredients. Mix together. Drop by spoonfuls onto ungreased baking sheet. Bake in 350°F oven for 8 to 10 minutes. Makes 6 dozen.

Pictured on page 53.

---

### Paré Pointer

*Cross a Pekingese and a Pomeranian and you will have a peeking pom.*

# Anzac Cookies

*These are crisp with a rich caramel color and taste. Popular "down under".*

| | |
|---|---|
| All-purpose flour | 1 cup |
| Granulated sugar | 1 cup |
| Rolled oats | 1 cup |
| Coconut | 1 cup |
| Butter (or hard margarine), melted | 1/2 cup |
| Golden syrup | 2 tbsp. |
| Baking soda | 1 tsp. |
| Boiling water | 1/4 cup |

Put flour, sugar, oats and coconut into mixing bowl. Stir together. Make a well in center.

Add butter and syrup to well.

Dissolve baking soda in water. Add to well. Mix. Drop by spoonfuls onto greased baking sheet. Bake in 350°F oven for about 8 to 10 minutes. Makes 3 dozen.

Pictured on page 53.

# Banana Oatmeal Cookies

*Banana with dates are a natural.*

| | |
|---|---|
| Butter (or hard margarine), softened | 3/4 cup |
| Granulated sugar | 1 cup |
| Large egg | 1 |
| Mashed banana | 1 cup |
| All-purpose flour | 1 1/2 cups |
| Salt | 1 tsp. |
| Baking soda | 1/2 tsp. |
| Cinnamon | 1 tsp. |
| Nutmeg | 1/4 tsp. |
| Rolled oats | 1 3/4 cups |
| Chopped nuts | 1/2 cup |
| Chopped dates | 1 cup |

(continued on next page)

Drop Cookies

Cream butter and sugar together well. Beat in egg. Add banana.

Stir remaining ingredients together and add. Mix well. Drop by spoonfuls onto greased baking sheet. Bake in 400°F oven for 10 to 12 minutes. Makes 4 1/2 dozen.

Pictured on page 89.

# Raisin Nut Drops

*These can be dropped or rolled into balls. They are moist, chewy, good.*

| | |
|---|---|
| Butter (or hard margarine), softened | 1 cup |
| Granulated sugar | 1 cup |
| Brown sugar, packed | 1 cup |
| Large eggs | 2 |
| Vanilla | 1 tsp. |
| Rum flavoring | 1 tsp. |
| Raisins, ground | 1 cup |
| Walnuts, ground | 1 cup |
| Rolled oats, ground | 1 cup |
| All-purpose flour | 2 1/4 cups |
| Baking soda | 1 1/2 tsp. |
| Salt | 1/4 tsp. |

In large bowl, cream butter and both sugars together. Beat in eggs 1 at a time. Add vanilla and rum flavoring.

Put raisins, walnuts and rolled oats through grinder or use food processor. Add to batter and mix in.

Stir flour, baking soda and salt together and mix in. Either drop from spoon or roll into small balls and place on greased baking sheet. Bake in 350°F oven for 7 to 8 minutes. Makes 6 dozen.

Pictured on page 71.

# Krunchy Krisps

*Crispy and crunchy. A good cookie jar filler.*

| | |
|---|---|
| Butter (or hard margarine), softened | 1 cup |
| Granulated sugar | 3/4 cup |
| Brown sugar, packed | 3/4 cup |
| Large eggs | 2 |
| Vanilla | 1 tsp. |
| All-purpose flour | 1 1/2 cups |
| Rolled oats | 1 1/2 cups |
| Coconut | 1/2 cup |
| Cinnamon | 1 tsp. |
| Baking powder | 1 tsp. |
| Baking soda | 1/2 tsp. |

Cream butter and both sugars together in mixing bowl. Beat in eggs and vanilla.

Stir in remaining ingredients. Drop by spoonfuls onto lightly greased cookie sheet. Bake in 375°F oven for about 10 minutes until browned. Makes about 5 dozen.

Pictured on page 125.

Drop Cookies

# Spicy Oatmeal Cookies

*These cookies are chewy and rich in color.*

| | |
|---|---|
| Butter (or hard margarine), softened | 1/2 cup |
| Granulated sugar | 1 cup |
| Large eggs | 2 |
| Molasses | 1/3 cup |
| All-purpose flour | 1 3/4 cups |
| Baking soda | 1 tsp. |
| Salt | 1/2 tsp. |
| Cinnamon | 1 1/2 tsp. |
| Raisins | 1 cup |
| Chopped nuts | 1/2 cup |
| Rolled oats | 2 cups |

Cream butter and sugar together. Beat in eggs 1 at a time. Add molasses.

Add remaining ingredients. Mix well. Drop by spoonfuls onto greased baking sheet. Bake in 350°F oven for 8 to 10 minutes. Makes about 5 dozen.

Pictured on page 89.

# Orange Cookies

*These contain raisins for added goodness.*

| | |
|---|---|
| Butter (or hard margarine), softened | 1/2 cup |
| Granulated sugar | 1 cup |
| Large eggs | 2 |
| Orange flavoring | 2 tsp. |
| Milk | 1/4 cup |
| All-purpose flour | 2 cups |
| Baking powder | 2 tsp. |
| Grated orange rind | 1 tbsp. |
| Raisins | 1 cup |

Cream butter and sugar together. Beat in eggs 1 at a time. Add orange flavoring and milk.

Add flour, baking powder, orange rind and raisins. Mix well. Drop by spoonfuls onto greased cookie sheet. Bake in 375°F oven for 8 to 10 minutes. Makes 3 1/2 dozen.

Pictured on page 53.

Drop Cookies

# Hermits

*One of the best known drop cookies. Cookie jars are*
*filled with these for after school snacks.*

| | |
|---|---|
| Butter (or hard margarine), softened | 1 cup |
| Brown sugar, packed | 1 1/2 cups |
| Large eggs | 3 |
| Vanilla | 1 tsp. |
| All-purpose flour | 3 cups |
| Baking powder | 1 tsp. |
| Baking soda | 1 tsp. |
| Salt | 1/2 tsp. |
| Cinnamon | 1 tsp. |
| Nutmeg | 1/2 tsp. |
| Allspice | 1/4 tsp. |
| Raisins | 1 cup |
| Chopped dates | 1 cup |
| Chopped nuts | 2/3 cup |

Cream butter and sugar together. Beat in eggs 1 at a time. Add vanilla.

Measure in remaining ingredients. Mix well. Drop onto greased baking sheet by heaping teaspoonfuls. Bake in 375°F oven for 6 to 8 minutes. Makes 4 1/2 dozen.

Pictured on page 125.

# Macaroons

*Chewy little stacks. Use the longest coconut you can find.*

| | |
|---|---|
| Egg whites (large) | 3 |
| Granulated sugar | 3/4 cup |
| Cornstarch | 2 tbsp. |
| Salt | 1/8 tsp. |
| Coconut, long threaded (approximately 2/3 lb.) | 4 cups |

In top of double boiler on counter, beat egg whites until stiff and dry. Place over boiling water.

(continued on next page)

Drop Cookies

Stir sugar, cornstarch and salt together. Add to whites. Stir to mix. Cook until crust forms around edge, about 5 minutes. Remove from heat.

Add coconut to thicken. Shape into balls. Drop by spoonfuls onto greased baking sheet. Bake in 350°F oven for about 12 to 15 minutes until slightly browned. Makes about 3 1/2 dozen cookies.

Pictured on page 53.

# Honey Oatmeal Cookies

*Soft and golden, studded with raisins.*

| | |
|---|---|
| Butter (or hard margarine), softened | 3/4 cup |
| Granulated sugar | 1/2 cup |
| Soft honey | 1/2 cup |
| Large egg | 1 |
| Vanilla | 1 tsp. |
| Rolled oats | 2 cups |
| All-purpose flour | 1 1/4 cups |
| Baking soda | 1 tsp. |
| Salt | 1/2 tsp. |
| Raisins | 1 cup |

Cream butter, sugar and honey together well. Beat in egg and vanilla.

Add remaining ingredients. Mix well. Drop by spoonfuls onto greased baking sheet. Bake in 350°F oven for 12 to 15 minutes. Makes 4 dozen.

**Variation:** Add 1 tbsp. grated orange rind.

**Variation:** Add 1 tbsp. cinnamon and 1 tbsp. grated lemon rind.

Pictured on page 89.

# Granola Chips

*With cereal, raisins and rolled oats, this is a nutritious cookie.*

| | |
|---|---|
| Butter (or hard margarine), softened | 1 cup |
| Granulated sugar | 3/4 cup |
| Brown sugar, packed | 3/4 cup |
| Large eggs | 2 |
| Vanilla | 1 tsp. |
| All-purpose flour | 1 1/2 cups |
| Granola | 2 cups |
| Rolled oats | 1 cup |
| Baking powder | 1 tsp. |
| Salt | 1/4 tsp. |
| Raisins | 1 cup |
| Semisweet chocolate chips | 1 cup |

Cream butter and both sugars together well. Beat in eggs 1 at a time. Add vanilla.

Add remaining ingredients. Stir. Drop by spoonfuls onto greased cookie sheet. Bake in 350°F oven for 10 to 12 minutes. Makes 7 dozen.

Pictured on page 35.

# Meringues

*Food for the angels. Shattery-crisp with chocolate chips added.*

| | |
|---|---|
| Egg whites (large) | 2 |
| Cream of tartar | 1/4 tsp. |
| Vanilla | 1 tsp. |
| Granulated sugar | 3/4 cup |
| Semisweet chocolate chips | 1 cup |
| Chopped pecans or walnuts | 1 cup |

Beat egg whites, cream of tartar and vanilla together until soft peaks form.

Add sugar gradually beating until stiff.

Fold in chocolate chips and pecans. Drop by teaspoonfuls onto greased cookie sheet. Bake in 300°F oven for 15 to 20 minutes. Makes 2 1/2 dozen.

Pictured on page 143.

Drop Cookies

# Chocolate Chippers

*These chocolate chip cookies are tops. A drop cookie that doesn't flatten too much.*

| | |
|---|---|
| Butter (or hard margarine), softened | 1 cup |
| Brown sugar, packed | 1 1/2 cups |
| Large eggs | 2 |
| Vanilla | 1 tsp. |
| All-purpose flour | 2 cups |
| Cornstarch | 1/4 cup |
| Salt | 3/4 tsp. |
| Baking soda | 1 tsp. |
| Semisweet chocolate chips | 2 cups |
| Chopped walnuts (optional) | 1 cup |

Cream butter and sugar together. Beat in eggs 1 at a time. Add vanilla.

Stir flour, cornstarch, salt and baking soda together and add. Stir in chips and nuts. Drop by spoonfuls onto greased baking sheet. Bake in 350°F oven for 10 to 15 minutes. Makes 5 1/2 dozen.

Pictured on page 35.

# Chocolate Drops

*A soft, dark cookie.*

| | |
|---|---|
| Butter (or hard margarine), softened | 1/2 cup |
| Granulated sugar | 1 cup |
| Large egg | 1 |
| Cocoa | 1/2 cup |
| Milk | 1/4 cup |
| Vanilla | 1 tsp. |
| All-purpose flour | 1 3/4 cups |
| Baking powder | 1 tsp. |
| Salt | 1/2 tsp. |
| Chopped nuts (optional) | 1/2 cup |

Cream butter and sugar together. Beat in egg. Stir in cocoa, milk and vanilla.

Stir flour, baking powder and salt together and add along with nuts. Mix well. Drop by spoonfuls onto greased pan. Bake in 375°F oven for 10 to 12 minutes. Makes 5 dozen.

Pictured on page 143.

# Frog Eyes

*A good butter cookie that is colorful—eaten by young or old.*

| | |
|---|---|
| Butter (or hard margarine), softened | 1 cup |
| Brown sugar, packed | 1 cup |
| Granulated sugar | 1/2 cup |
| Large eggs | 2 |
| Vanilla | 2 tsp. |
| All-purpose flour | 2 1/4 cups |
| Baking soda | 1 tsp. |
| Salt | 1 tsp. |
| Candy-coated chocolate bits, such as M & M's | 1/2 cup |
| Candy-coated chocolate bits, such as M & M's | 1 cup |

Cream butter and both sugars together. Beat in eggs 1 at a time. Mix in vanilla.

Add flour, baking soda, salt and first amount of chocolate bits. Mix well. Drop by spoonfuls onto ungreased cookie sheet.

Press remaining candies on top of cookies using 2 or 3 per cookie. Bake in 375°F oven for 8 to 10 minutes until golden brown. Makes 4 dozen.

Pictured on page 35.

## Paré Pointer
*A karate school is one place where you don't knock before entering.*

# Best Drop Cookies

*Good natural flavor with no spices added. Extra good.*

| | |
|---|---|
| Butter (or hard margarine), softened | 1 cup |
| Brown sugar, packed | 1 1/2 cups |
| Large eggs | 2 |
| Vanilla | 1 tsp. |
| Dates, cut up | 1 lb. |
| All-purpose flour | 2 cups |
| Rolled oats | 1 cup |
| Coconut | 1/2 cup |
| Baking soda | 1 tsp. |
| Chopped walnuts | 1/2 cup |
| Candied cherries, quartered, for color (optional) | 1/2 cup |

Cream butter and sugar well. Beat in eggs and vanilla.

Add remaining ingredients. Mix well. Drop by spoonfuls onto greased baking sheet. Bake in 350°F oven for 10 to 12 minutes. Makes 5 dozen.

Pictured on page 71.

# Soft Molasses Drops

*An old-time recipe, these are moist and spicy.*

| | |
|---|---|
| All-purpose flour | 3 1/2 cups |
| Granulated sugar | 3/4 cup |
| Ginger | 1 tsp. |
| Cinnamon | 1 tsp. |
| Salt | 1/2 tsp. |
| Molasses | 3/4 cup |
| Butter (or hard margarine), softened | 3/4 cup |
| Large egg | 1 |
| Baking soda | 1 1/2 tsp. |
| Hot coffee (or hot milk) | 1/2 cup |

Measure first 8 ingredients in order given into mixing bowl.

Stir baking soda into hot coffee. Add and beat dough until thoroughly blended. Drop by tablespoons onto greased cookie sheet. Bake in 375°F oven for 10 to 12 minutes. Makes 5 dozen.

Pictured on page 89.

Drop Cookies

# Oatmeal Molasses Cookies

*Rich and chewy.*

| | |
|---|---|
| All-purpose flour | 1 1/2 cups |
| Granulated sugar | 1/2 cup |
| Brown sugar | 1/2 cup |
| Baking soda | 1 tsp. |
| Salt | 1/2 tsp. |
| Ginger | 1/2 tsp. |
| Cloves | 1/4 tsp. |
| Butter (or hard margarine), softened | 3/4 cup |
| Molasses | 1/4 cup |
| Large egg | 1 |
| Rolled oats | 3/4 cup |

Measure first 10 ingredients into mixing bowl. Beat well.

Stir in rolled oats. Drop by spoonfuls onto greased baking sheet. Bake in 375°F oven for 8 to 10 minutes until browned. Makes 32 large cookies.

Pictured on page 125.

# Fruit Cocktail Cookies

*Probably this is the softest of all fruit cookies.*

| | |
|---|---|
| Butter (or hard margarine), softened | 1/2 cup |
| Granulated sugar | 1/2 cup |
| Large egg | 1 |
| Vanilla | 1/2 tsp. |
| Fruit cocktail, drained | 14 oz. |
| All-purpose flour | 2 cups |
| Baking soda | 1 tsp. |
| Salt | 1/2 tsp. |
| Cinnamon | 1/2 tsp. |
| Raisins | 1/2 cup |
| Chopped walnuts | 1/2 cup |

Cream butter and sugar together. Beat in egg and vanilla. Stir in fruit.

Add remaining ingredients. Stir together. Drop by spoonfuls onto greased baking sheet. Bake in 350°F oven until golden, about 10 minutes. Makes 4 dozen.

Pictured on page 89.

Drop Cookies

# Oatmeal Chip Cookies

*Chocolate chips in a favorite oatmeal base produce
the ultimate cookie. A great favorite.*

| | |
|---|---|
| Butter (or hard margarine), softened | 1 cup |
| Brown sugar, packed | 2 cups |
| Large eggs | 2 |
| Vanilla | 1 tsp. |
| All-purpose flour | 2 cups |
| Baking powder | 1 tsp. |
| Baking soda | 1/2 tsp. |
| Rolled oats | 2 cups |
| Semisweet chocolate chips | 2 cups |
| Medium coconut | 3/4 cup |

Cream butter and sugar together. Beat in eggs 1 at a time. Add vanilla.

Add remaining ingredients. Mix well. Drop by spoonfuls onto greased baking sheet. Bake in 350°F oven for about 8 to 10 minutes. Makes 5 dozen.

**OATMEAL CHIP PIZZA:** Press 3 cups dough into greased 12 inch pizza pan. Sprinkle with semisweet and butterscotch chips, nuts, coconut, candy-coated chocolate (M & M's), and any other treat you like. Allow a bit more time to bake.

Pictured on page 71.

---

## Paré Pointer

*The little firefly didn't stay because when you've got to glow, you've got to glow.*

# Cherry Coconut Drops

*This is golden brown with a light center. There is a subtle lemon flavor with cherries adding greatly to the festive look.*

| | |
|---|---|
| Butter (or hard margarine), softened | 1 cup |
| Granulated sugar | 1 cup |
| Large eggs | 3 |
| Sour cream | 1/2 cup |
| Lemon flavoring | 1 1/2 tsp. |
| Grated orange rind | 1 tsp. |
| All-purpose flour | 3 1/4 cups |
| Baking powder | 1 tsp. |
| Baking soda | 1/2 tsp. |
| Salt | 1 tsp. |
| Chopped candied cherries | 1/2 cup |
| Shredded coconut | 1 cup |

Cream butter and sugar together. Beat in eggs 1 at a time. Add sour cream, lemon flavoring and orange rind.

Mix in remaining ingredients in order given. Drop from teaspoon onto greased cookie sheet. Bake in 400°F oven for 8 to 12 minutes. Makes about 6 dozen.

Pictured on page 17.

# Coconut Crumb Cookies

*Bread crumbs replace flour in these but no one would ever guess.*

| | |
|---|---|
| Large eggs | 2 |
| Granulated sugar (or brown) | 1 cup |
| Coconut | 1 cup |
| Dry bread crumbs | 1 cup |

Beat eggs until frothy.

Stir in sugar, coconut and crumbs. Drop by spoonfuls onto greased baking sheet. Batter will be stiff. You may have to shape drops a bit with your hand. Bake in 350°F oven until browned, 10 to 15 minutes. Makes 2 1/2 dozen.

Pictured on page 71.

# Cookies

*...e added or not as wished.*

|  |  |
|---|---|
|  | 1 cup |
|  | 1 cup |
|  | 1 |
|  | 1 tsp. |
|  | 2 cups |
|  | 1 tsp. |
|  | 1/8 tsp. |

...egg and vanilla.

...well. Drop by teaspoonfuls
...oven for 6 to 8 minutes.

...dozen.

Pictured on page 71.

# Ragged Robins

*Quick and easy. Just combine beaten egg whites with other ingredients.*

| | |
|---|---|
| Egg whites (large), room temperature | 2 |
| Granulated sugar | 1/2 cup |
| Vanilla | 1 tsp. |
| Chopped dates | 1 cup |
| Chopped nuts | 1 cup |
| Cornflakes | 2 cups |
| Candied chopped cherries | 1/4 cup |

Beat egg whites until soft peaks form. Gradually beat in sugar until stiff. Add vanilla.

Fold in dates, nuts, cornflakes and cherries. Drop by spoonfuls onto greased baking sheet. Bake in 325°F oven for about 15 minutes. Makes 3 dozen.

Pictured on page 35.

# Boiled Raisin Cookies

*Spicy and moist, this is a different method of making good drop cookies.*

| | |
|---|---|
| Raisins | 2 cups |
| Water | 1 cup |
| Butter (or hard margarine), softened | 1 cup |
| Brown sugar, packed | 1 cup |
| Granulated sugar | 1 cup |
| Large eggs | 2 |
| All-purpose flour | 3 cups |
| Baking soda | 1 tsp. |
| Salt | 3/4 tsp. |
| Cinnamon | 1 1/4 tsp. |
| Nutmeg | 1/2 tsp. |
| Allspice | 1/4 tsp. |
| Rolled oats | 2 cups |
| Chopped nuts | 1/2 cup |

Bring raisins and water to a boil in small saucepan. Boil 5 minutes. Cool.

Cream butter and both sugars together. Beat in eggs 1 at a time.

Stir remaining ingredients together and add to creamed mixture. Pour in raisins and juice. Mix well. Drop by spoonfuls onto greased baking sheet. Bake in 350°F oven for 12 to 15 minutes. Makes 6 dozen.

Pictured on page 89.

***Paré Pointer***
*The clock was removed from the library. It tocked too much.*

Drop Cookies

# Date Nut Cookies

*This presents dates in a tasty, moist cookie.*

| | |
|---|---|
| Butter (or hard margarine), softened | 1 cup |
| Granulated sugar | 1 cup |
| Large eggs | 3 |
| Vanilla | 1 tsp. |
| All-purpose flour | 2 cups |
| Baking soda | 1 tsp. |
| Salt | 1/2 tsp. |
| Chopped dates | 1 lb. |
| Chopped walnuts | 1 cup |

Cream butter and sugar together. Beat in eggs 1 at a time. Add vanilla.

Mix in remaining ingredients. Drop by spoonfuls onto greased cookie sheet. Bake in 350°F oven for 10 to 12 minutes. Makes 6 dozen.

Pictured on page 53.

# Praline Lace

*These look similar to Lace Cookies, page 46, however they contain no eggs or rolled oats.*

| | |
|---|---|
| Corn syrup | 2/3 cup |
| Butter (or hard margarine), softened | 2/3 cup |
| Brown sugar, packed | 2/3 cup |
| All-purpose flour | 1 cup |
| Ground almonds | 1 cup |

Combine syrup, butter and sugar in saucepan. Bring to a boil while stirring continually over medium heat. Remove from heat.

Stir in flour and almonds. Drop in scant 1 tsp. amounts onto greased cookie sheet. Bake in 375°F oven for 4 to 5 minutes until edges brown. Let stand on pan for about 2 minutes before removing. Makes 5 dozen.

Pictured on page 143.

# Filbert Fingers

*Dainty and elegant describe these scrumptious cookies. Pretty as a picture.*

| | |
|---|---|
| Butter (not hard margarine), softened | 1 cup |
| Brown sugar, packed | 3/4 cup |
| All-purpose flour | 2 1/2 cups |
| Milk | 2 tbsp. |
| Ground filberts | 1 cup |
| Semi-sweet chocolate squares | 2 x 1 oz. |
| Grated parowax (paraffin) | 2 tbsp. |

Mix butter, sugar, flour and milk together. Form into a ball and knead until soft and pliable.

Mix in nuts. Shape into fingers. Place on ungreased baking sheet. Bake in 375°F oven for about 10 minutes. Cool.

Melt chocolate and parowax in saucepan over hot water. Dip ends of fingers. Place on waxed paper to set. Makes 6 1/2 dozen.

Pictured on page 143.

# Cake Mix Cookies

*Make from a cake mix from the shelf. Actually like a peanut butter cookie.*

| | |
|---|---|
| Smooth peanut butter | 1 cup |
| Butter (or hard margarine), softened | 1/4 cup |
| Water | 1/4 cup |
| Large eggs | 2 |
| Yellow cake mix, 2 layer size | 1 |

Combine peanut butter, butter, water and eggs in bowl. Mix together.

Add cake mix. Stir well. Drop by teaspoonfuls onto ungreased cookie sheet. Press with floured fork in criss-cross style to flatten. Bake in 375°F oven for about 10 minutes. Makes about 4 dozen.

Pictured on page 35.

Drop Cookies

# Oatmeal Raisin Cookies

*A moist drop-type cookie.*

| | |
|---|---|
| Butter (or hard margarine), softened | 1 cup |
| Brown sugar, packed | 1 cup |
| Large egg | 1 |
| Vanilla | 1 tsp. |
| All-purpose flour | 1 1/2 cups |
| Baking soda | 1 tsp. |
| Salt | 1/4 tsp. |
| Rolled oats | 1 1/4 cups |
| Raisins | 1 cup |

Cream butter and sugar together. Beat in egg and vanilla.

Add remaining ingredients. Mix well. Drop by spoonfuls onto greased cookie sheet. Bake in 350°F oven for 8 to 10 minutes. Makes 3 1/2 dozen.

Pictured on page 53.

# Fruit Drops

*These light-colored cookies are flavored with raisins, cherries and coconut. No spices in these.*

| | |
|---|---|
| Butter (or hard margarine), softened | 1 cup |
| Brown sugar, packed | 3/4 cup |
| Large egg | 1 |
| Vanilla | 1 tsp. |
| Maraschino cherry juice | 2 tbsp. |
| All-purpose flour | 2 cups |
| Baking powder | 1/2 tsp. |
| Salt | 1/4 tsp. |
| Raisins or currants | 1/2 cup |
| Chopped dates | 1/2 cup |
| Maraschino cherries, quartered | 1/2 cup |
| Shredded coconut | 1/2 cup |

Cream butter and sugar well. Beat in egg, vanilla and cherry juice.

Measure in remaining ingredients. Stir to mix. Drop by spoonfuls onto greased cookie sheet. Bake in 375°F oven for 10 to 12 minutes. Makes 3 1/2 dozen.

Pictured on page 17.

# Spicy Dads

*A spicy version of the commercial variety.*

| | |
|---|---|
| Butter (or hard margarine), softened | 1 cup |
| Granulated sugar | 1 cup |
| Brown sugar, packed | 1/2 cup |
| Large egg | 1 |
| Molasses | 2 tbsp. |
| Vanilla | 1 tsp. |
| All-purpose flour | 1 1/2 cups |
| Rolled oats | 1 1/2 cups |
| Coconut | 1 cup |
| Baking powder | 1 tsp. |
| Baking soda | 1 tsp. |
| Cinnamon | 1 tsp. |
| Nutmeg | 1 tsp. |
| Allspice | 1 tsp. |

Cream butter and both sugars together. Beat in egg. Add molasses and vanilla.

Stir remaining ingredients together and add. Mix well. Drop by spoonfuls onto greased baking sheet. Press with floured fork. Bake in 300°F oven until golden, about 12 minutes. Makes 6 dozen.

Pictured on page 71.

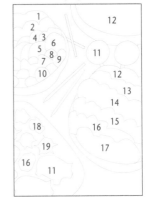

# Lemonade Cookies

*Made with concentrated lemonade, these are soft and moist with just a hint of lemon.*

| | |
|---|---|
| Butter (or hard margarine), softened | 1 cup |
| Granulated sugar | 1 cup |
| Large eggs | 2 |
| Frozen concentrated lemonade,<br>thawed and halved | 6 oz. |
| All-purpose flour | 3 cups |
| Baking soda | 1 tsp. |
| Salt | 1/2 tsp. |

Concentrated lemonade for garnish

Cream butter and sugar together. Beat in eggs 1 at a time. Add 3 oz. concentrated lemonade.

Stir flour, baking soda and salt together and add. Mix well. Drop by spoonfuls onto greased cookie sheet. Bake in 375°F oven for 10 to 12 minutes until light brown.

Brush tops of cookies with concentrated lemonade. Makes about 5 dozen.

**Note:** If frozen concentrated lemonade is not available, stir 1/2 cup hot water with 1/4 cup lemon juice and 1/4 cup granulated sugar until mixed and sugar is dissolved. Use as directed above.

Pictured on page 35.

# Date Meringues

*These actually melt in your mouth.*

| | |
|---|---|
| Egg whites (large), room temperature | 2 |
| Icing (confectioner's) sugar | 1 cup |
| Chopped dates | 1 cup |

In mixing bowl beat egg whites until soft peaks form. Add sugar gradually continuing to beat until stiff. Fold in dates. Drop by spoonfuls onto greased cookie sheet. Bake in 300°F oven for about 12 to 15 minutes. Makes 2 dozen.

Pictured on page 143.

# Bran Cereal Cookies

*These chewy cookies are good with or without cinnamon.*

| | |
|---|---|
| Butter (or hard margarine), softened | 1 cup |
| Granulated sugar | 1 cup |
| Large eggs | 2 |
| Vanilla | 1 1/2 tsp. |
| All-purpose flour | 1 1/2 cups |
| Baking soda | 1 tsp. |
| Salt | 1/2 tsp. |
| Cinnamon (optional) | 1 tsp. |
| All bran cereal | 1 1/2 cups |
| Chopped nuts | 1 cup |

Cream butter and sugar together. Beat in eggs 1 at a time. Add vanilla.

Measure in remaining ingredients. Mix well. Drop by spoonfuls onto greased baking sheet. Bake in 375°F oven for 12 to 14 minutes. Makes 4 dozen.

Pictured on page 35.

# Chocolate Nuggets

*These are incredible cookies. They are extra rich and extra chocolaty and brownie-like. Make for a special treat when cost is no object.*

| | |
|---|---|
| Semisweet chocolate chips | 2 cups |
| Butter (or hard margarine) | 1/4 cup |
| Sweetened condensed milk | 14 oz. |
| Granulated sugar | 1/4 cup |
| Vanilla | 1 tsp. |
| All-purpose flour | 1 cup |
| Chopped nuts (optional) | 1/2 cup |

Melt first 5 ingredients together in saucepan over medium heat. Stir often.

Add flour and nuts. Mix well. Drop by spoonfuls onto greased cookie sheet. Bake in 350°F oven for about 10 to 12 minutes. Cookies will be soft. Makes 6 dozen.

Pictured on page 143.

Drop Cookies

# Oatmeal Cookies

*So caramelly tasting. A great cookie jar type.*

| | |
|---|---|
| Large eggs | 2 |
| Brown sugar, packed | 1 cup |
| Granulated sugar | 1/2 cup |
| Cooking oil | 1 cup |
| Vanilla | 1 tsp. |
| Baking soda | 1 tsp. |
| Hot water | 1 tbsp. |
| Rolled oats | 2 cups |
| All-purpose flour | 1 1/2 cups |
| Salt | 1 tsp. |

Beat eggs in mixing bowl until frothy. Beat in both sugars. Add cooking oil and vanilla.

Dissolve baking soda in hot water. Stir in.

Add oats, flour and salt. Stir well. Drop by spoonfuls onto greased baking sheet. Bake in 350°F oven for about 8 minutes. Makes 3 1/2 dozen.

Pictured on page 71.

**RAISIN OATMEAL:** Add 1 cup raisins. If you would like spice too, add 1 tsp. cinnamon, 1/4 tsp. nutmeg and 1/4 tsp. allspice. Nuts are optional, 1/2 cup.

**LOLLIPOPS:** To make oatmeal lollipops see method in Rolled Ginger Cookies recipe on page 93.

# Peanut Cereal Stacks

*Quick to prepare this firm, chewy cookie.*

| | |
|---|---|
| Smooth peanut butter | 1/2 cup |
| Granulated sugar | 1/2 cup |
| Evaporated milk | 1/4 cup |
| Cornflakes | 2 1/2 cups |

Put peanut butter, sugar and milk into bowl. Blend together until smooth. Add cornflakes. Mix well to coat evenly. Drop by teaspoonfuls onto ungreased cookie sheet. Bake in 375°F oven until browned, about 6 minutes. Makes about 2 1/2 dozen.

Pictured on page 89.

Drop Cookies

# Chocolate Cream Drops

*A very mellow chocolate flavor. Tops.*

| | |
|---|---|
| Butter (or hard margarine), softened | 1 cup |
| Cream cheese, softened | 4 oz. |
| Granulated sugar | 1 1/2 cups |
| Large egg | 1 |
| Milk | 2 tbsp. |
| Vanilla | 1/2 tsp. |
| Unsweetened chocolate squares, melted | 2 x 1 oz. |
| Cake flour | 2 1/2 cups |
| Baking powder | 1 1/2 tsp. |
| Salt | 1/4 tsp. |
| Chopped walnuts | 1/2 cup |

Cream butter, cheese and sugar together well. Beat in egg, milk, vanilla and chocolate.

Stir remaining ingredients together and add. Mix well. Drop by spoonfuls onto greased baking sheet. Bake in 350°F oven for 10 to 12 minutes. To have a continuing supply of these, pack in layers in plastic container while still a bit warm, with plastic wrap in between layers. Cover with lid and freeze. When removed to serve, they are moist and luscious. Makes 5 dozen.

Pictured on page 89.

# Pineapple Cookies

*A refreshing fruity flavor.*

| | |
|---|---|
| Butter (or hard margarine), softened | 1/2 cup |
| Granulated sugar | 1/2 cup |
| Large egg | 1 |
| Vanilla | 1 tsp. |
| Crushed pineapple, drained | 1/2 cup |
| All-purpose flour | 2 cups |
| Baking powder | 1 tsp. |
| Baking soda | 1 tsp. |
| Salt | 1/2 tsp. |
| Granulated sugar | 1 tbsp. |
| Nutmeg | 1/4 tsp. |

*(continued on next page)*

Drop Cookies

Cream butter and first amount of sugar together well. Beat in egg. Stir in vanilla and pineapple.

Add flour, baking powder, soda and salt. Stir. Drop by spoonfuls onto ungreased baking sheet.

Mix second amount of sugar and nutmeg together. Sprinkle on top of unbaked cookies. Bake in 375°F oven for about 8 to 10 minutes. Makes about 3 dozen.

Pictured on page 53.

# Fruit Jumbles

*A fruity spice-colored cookie. Makes a batch large enough to exchange with friends.*

| | |
|---|---|
| Candied cherries, chopped | 1 cup |
| Chopped dates | 1 cup |
| Chopped nuts | 1 cup |
| Raisins | 1 cup |
| Cut mixed peel | 1/4 cup |
| All-purpose flour | 1/2 cup |
| Butter (or hard margarine), softened | 1 1/2 cups |
| Brown sugar, packed | 1 cup |
| Granulated sugar | 1 cup |
| Large eggs | 3 |
| All-purpose flour | 3 1/2 cups |
| Baking powder | 1 tsp. |
| Baking soda | 1 tsp. |
| Salt | 1 tsp. |
| Cinnamon | 1 tsp. |
| Cloves | 1/8 tsp. |

Measure first 6 ingredients into bowl. Mix thoroughly.

In another bowl cream butter and both sugars together. Add eggs 1 at a time, beating after each addition.

Stir remaining ingredients together. Add and mix well. Add fruit. Mix together. Drop by spoonfuls onto greased baking sheet. Bake in 375°F oven for 8 to 10 minutes. Makes 10 dozen.

Pictured on page 53.

# Carrot Cookies

*A moist cookie that uses leftover or fresh carrots. These contain rolled oats.*

| | |
|---|---|
| Butter (or hard margarine), softened | 1/2 cup |
| Granulated sugar | 1 cup |
| Large egg | 1 |
| Cooked, mashed carrots (or fresh, grated) | 1 cup |
| Milk | 1/3 cup |
| Vanilla | 1 tsp. |
| All-purpose flour | 2 cups |
| Rolled oats | 2 cups |
| Baking powder | 2 tsp. |
| Salt | 1/4 tsp. |
| Cinnamon | 1 tsp. |
| Raisins | 1 cup |

Cream butter and sugar well. Beat in egg. Mix in carrot, milk and vanilla.

Add remaining ingredients. Mix well. Drop by spoonfuls onto greased cookie sheet. Bake in 375°F oven for about 12 to 15 minutes until slightly browned. Frost if desired. Makes about 4 dozen.

## ICING

| | |
|---|---|
| Icing (confectioner's) sugar | 2 1/2 cups |
| Butter (or hard margarine), softened | 1/3 cup |
| Prepared orange juice | 2–3 tbsp. |
| Grated orange rind | 1 1/2 tbsp. |

Beat all together adding more or less orange juice to make icing proper consistency. Ice or dip cookies into icing.

Pictured on page 35.

*Paré Pointer*
*You have to know all the angles to pass a geometry test.*

Drop Cookies

# Christmas Cookies

*These are moist with a Brazil nut flavor. An attractive cookie.*

| | |
|---|---|
| Butter (or hard margarine), softened | 1 cup |
| Brown sugar, packed | 3/4 cup |
| Large egg | 1 |
| All-purpose flour | 1 1/4 cups |
| Salt | 1/2 tsp. |
| Cinnamon | 1/2 tsp. |
| Baking soda | 1/2 tsp. |
| Chopped dates | 1/2 cup |
| Glazed cherries, chopped | 1/2 cup |
| Candied pineapple slices, chopped | 2 |
| Chopped walnuts | 1 cup |
| Slivered almonds | 1/2 cup |
| Brazil nuts, chopped | 1/2 cup |

Cream butter and sugar together. Beat in egg.

Stir flour, salt, cinnamon and baking soda together and add. Mix to combine.

Add remaining ingredients. Mix well. Drop by spoonfuls onto greased cookie sheet. Bake in 350°F oven for 10 to 15 minutes. Makes 5 dozen.

Pictured on page 17.

# Cornflake Macaroons

*These are both crispy and chewy.*

| | |
|---|---|
| Egg whites (large), room temperature | 2 |
| Granulated sugar | 3/4 cup |
| Vanilla | 1/2 tsp. |
| Cornflakes | 2 cups |
| Chopped nuts | 1/2 cup |
| Shredded coconut | 1 cup |

In mixing bowl beat egg whites until soft peaks form. Add sugar gradually beating until stiff. Add vanilla.

Fold in cornflakes, nuts and coconut. Drop by spoonfuls onto greased baking sheet. Bake in 325°F oven for 12 to 15 minutes. Makes 3 dozen.

Pictured on page 89.

Drop Cookies

# Gum Drops

*These are extra chewy with gum drops baked in them.*

| | |
|---|---|
| Butter (or hard margarine), softened | 1 cup |
| Brown sugar, packed | 1 cup |
| Granulated sugar | 1/4 cup |
| Large eggs | 2 |
| Vanilla | 1 tsp. |
| All-purpose flour | 1 1/2 cups |
| Baking powder | 1 tsp. |
| Baking soda | 1/2 tsp. |
| Salt | 1/2 tsp. |
| Rolled oats | 1 cup |
| Gum drops, cut up (no black) | 1 cup |
| Chopped nuts (optional) | 1/2 cup |

Cream butter and both sugars together. Beat in eggs 1 at a time. Add vanilla.

Add remaining ingredients. Mix well. Drop by spoonfuls onto ungreased baking sheet. Bake in 350°F oven for 12 to 14 minutes. Makes 4 dozen.

Pictured on cover.

# Almond Macaroons

*A shattery good Italian treat.*

| | |
|---|---|
| Egg whites (large), room temperature | 2 |
| Granulated sugar | 1 cup |
| Ground almonds | 1 cup |
| Cornstarch | 2 tbsp. |
| Almond flavoring | 1/4 tsp. |
| Maraschino cherries or almonds | |

Beat egg whites until soft peaks form. Add sugar gradually, beating until stiff.

Fold in almonds, cornstarch and flavoring. Drop by spoonfuls onto greased baking sheet, flattening slightly with finger if needed.

*(continued on next page)*

Drop Cookies

Place whole or half cherry or almond in center. These are also good without cherries or almonds. Bake in 325°F oven for about 15 minutes. Makes about 2 1/2 dozen.

Pictured on page 17.

# Rainbow Chip Cookies

*These delicious cookies contain no flour. Soft and chewy with candy-coated chocolate added. Makes a huge batch.*

| | |
|---|---|
| Smooth peanut butter | 6 cups |
| Butter (or hard margarine), softened | 2 cups |
| Brown sugar, packed | 6 cups |
| Granulated sugar | 4 cups |
| Large eggs | 12 |
| Vanilla | 1 tbsp. |
| Corn syrup | 1 tbsp. |
| Rolled oats | 18 cups |
| Baking soda | 8 tsp. |
| Semisweet chocolate chips | 2 cups |
| Candy-coated chocolate bits, such as M & M's | 2 cups |

In mixing bowl, cream peanut butter, butter, brown and granulated sugar together. Beat in eggs, 2 at a time. Mix in vanilla and syrup. Transfer to extra large container.

Mix in remaining ingredients. Drop by ice cream scoop onto greased pan. Flatten with hand. May be dropped by teaspoonfuls for a smaller cookie. Bake in 350°F oven for 10 to 12 minutes for large cookies and 7 to 8 minutes for small. Overbaking makes them hard. Makes 5 dozen, 3 inch cookies, 1 dozen, 5 inch cookies and 1 pizza cookie.

**PIZZA:** Use 3 cups cookie dough. Press into 12 inch pizza pan. Sprinkle with more semisweet chocolate chips, butterscotch chips, M & M's, cereal flakes, coconut, peanuts and any other things you fancy. Bake for 12 to 15 minutes. Serve in wedges, warm or cold.

Pictured on page 35.

# Lace Cookies

*When baked, these are full of holes giving them a lacy look. Fancy.*

| | |
|---|---|
| Butter (or hard margarine), melted | 3/4 cup |
| Granulated sugar | 3/4 cup |
| Brown sugar, packed | 3/4 cup |
| Large egg | 1 |
| Vanilla | 1 tsp. |
| Rolled oats | 1 1/2 cups |
| All-purpose flour | 1/4 cup |
| Baking powder | 1 tsp. |
| Salt | 1/4 tsp. |

In mixing bowl beat butter and both sugars well. Beat in egg and vanilla.

Add remaining ingredients. Mix. Drop by 1/2 tsp. onto greased cookie sheet. Bake in 375°F oven for about 4 minutes. Let stand 1 to 3 minutes before removing until they can be removed without tearing. Leave flat for a lacy appearance. Makes about 6 1/2 dozen.

Pictured on page 143.

# Quick Macaroons

*Fast to make these chewy cookies. May be made with or without cherries.*

| | |
|---|---|
| Shredded coconut | 2 1/2 cups |
| Sweetened condensed milk | 1/2 cup |
| Vanilla | 1 tsp. |
| Maraschino cherries | 6–12 |

Put first 3 ingredients into bowl. Mix well. Drop by spoonfuls onto greased baking sheet about 1 inch apart.

Top with 1/4 or 1/2 maraschino cherry. Bake in 350°F oven for 8 to 10 minutes. Remove immediately from baking sheet. Makes 2 dozen.

Pictured on page 17.

Drop Cookies

# Fruitcake Drops

*Raisins, currants, fruit and nuts combine to make fruited cookies
instead of fruitcake.*

| | |
|---|---|
| Golden raisins | 1/2 cup |
| Currants or raisins | 1/2 cup |
| Candied cut mixed fruit | 2 cups |
| Chopped pecans or walnuts | 1 cup |
| All-purpose flour | 1/2 cup |
| Butter (or hard margarine), softened | 1/2 cup |
| Granulated sugar | 3/4 cup |
| Large eggs | 2 |
| Vanilla | 1 tsp. |
| Brandy flavoring | 2 tsp. |
| All-purpose flour | 1 cup |
| Baking soda | 1 tsp. |
| Salt | 1/4 tsp. |
| Cinnamon | 1/2 tsp. |
| Nutmeg | 1/4 tsp. |

Measure first 5 ingredients into bowl. Stir well to coat. Set aside.

Cream butter and sugar together. Beat in eggs 1 at a time. Add vanilla and brandy flavoring.

Stir remaining ingredients together and add. Mix in fruit. Drop by spoonfuls onto greased baking sheet. Bake in 325°F oven for 15 to 20 minutes. Makes 5 dozen.

Pictured on page 17.

Pictured on page 17.

---

### Paré Pointer
*Did you know there are only twenty four letters in the alphabet?
E.T. went home.*

# Apple Cookies

*When these bake there is an aroma of apple pie. A soft drop cookie.*

| | |
|---|---|
| Butter (or hard margarine), softened | 1/2 cup |
| Brown sugar, packed | 1 1/2 cups |
| Large egg | 1 |
| All-purpose flour | 2 cups |
| Baking soda | 1 tsp. |
| Cinnamon | 1 tsp. |
| Cloves | 1/2 tsp. |
| Nutmeg | 1/2 tsp. |
| Salt | 1/2 tsp. |
| Apple, peeled and grated | 1 cup |
| Raisins | 1 cup |
| Chopped walnuts or pecans | 1 cup |
| Milk | 1/4 cup |

Put butter, sugar and egg into mixing bowl. Beat well until smooth.

Stir flour, baking soda, cinnamon, cloves, nutmeg and salt together and add. Mix.

Stir in remaining ingredients. Drop by teaspoonfuls onto greased baking sheet. Bake in 400°F oven for 8 to 10 minutes. When cool spread with Caramel or Vanilla Icing. Makes 5 dozen.

## CARAMEL ICING

| | |
|---|---|
| Butter (or hard margarine) | 2 tbsp. |
| Brown sugar, packed | 2 tbsp. |
| Icing (confectioner's) sugar | 3/4 cup |
| Milk | 4 tsp. |

Combine butter and sugar in small saucepan. Stir and bring to boil over medium heat. Simmer 2 minutes. Remove from heat.

Add icing sugar and milk. Add more milk or sugar if needed to make proper spreadng consistency. Ice cookies.

*(continued on next page)*

Drop Cookies

**VANILLA ICING**

| | |
|---|---|
| Icing (confectioner's) sugar | 3/4 cup |
| Butter (or hard margarine), softened | 2 tsp. |
| Vanilla | 1/8 tsp. |
| Milk | 1 tbsp. |

Mix all together adding more milk if needed to make spreading consistency. Ice cookies.

Pictured on page 125.

---

# Chocolate Softies

*Jazz these up with a bit of icing.*

| | |
|---|---|
| Butter (or hard margarine), softened | 1/2 cup |
| Granulated sugar | 1 cup |
| Large egg | 1 |
| Squares of unsweetened chocolate, melted | 2 x 1 oz. |
| Sour milk | 1/3 cup |
| Vanilla | 1 tsp. |
| All-purpose flour | 1 3/4 cups |
| Baking soda | 1/2 tsp. |
| Salt | 1/2 tsp. |
| Chopped walnuts (optional) | 1/2 cup |

Mix first 6 ingredients together well.

Stir in remaining ingredients. Drop by teaspoonfuls onto ungreased cookie sheet, allowing room for spreading. Bake in 400°F oven for about 8 to 10 minutes. When pressed slightly, it should leave no dent. Remove from cookie sheet. Cool. Makes 4 dozen.

**ICING**

| | |
|---|---|
| Icing (confectioner's) sugar | 1 1/4 cups |
| Cocoa | 1/3 cup |
| Butter (or hard margarine), softened | 3 tbsp. |
| Hot coffee or water | 5 tsp. |

Beat all together until smooth, adding a bit more liquid if needed to make proper spreading consistency. Ice cookies.

Pictured on cover.

Drop Cookies

# Zucchini Drops

*Little heaps of moist goodness. Lightly spiced.*

| | |
|---|---|
| Butter (or hard margarine), softened | 3/4 cup |
| Granulated sugar | 1 1/2 cups |
| Large eggs | 2 |
| Grated zucchini, unpeeled | 1 1/2 cups |
| Vanilla | 1 tsp. |
| All-purpose flour | 2 1/2 cups |
| Baking powder | 1 tsp. |
| Baking soda | 1 tsp. |
| Cinnamon | 1 1/2 tsp. |
| Salt | 1/2 tsp. |
| Raisins | 1 1/2 cups |
| Chopped walnuts | 1 cup |

Cream butter and sugar well. Beat in eggs 1 at a time. Add zucchini and vanilla.

Stir remaining ingredients together and add. Mix well. Drop by spoonfuls onto greased baking sheet. Bake in 350°F oven for 12 to 15 minutes. Makes 5 dozen.

Pictured on page 89.

# Carrot Spice Cookies

*For a healthy variation, use whole wheat flour to replace half of the white.*

| | |
|---|---|
| Butter (or hard margarine), softened | 1/2 cup |
| Brown sugar, packed | 1 cup |
| Large egg | 1 |
| Grated carrot | 1 1/2 cups |
| All-purpose flour or whole wheat | 2 cups |
| Baking powder | 1 tsp. |
| Baking soda | 1/2 tsp. |
| Salt | 1/4 tsp. |
| Cinnamon | 1/2 tsp. |

*(continued on next page)*

Drop Cookies

Cream butter and sugar well. Beat in egg. Stir in carrot.

Stir remaining ingredients together and add. Mix well. Drop by spoonfuls onto greased cookie sheet. Bake in 350°F oven for 10 to 12 minutes. Makes about 3 dozen.

Pictured on page 89.

# Thresher's Cookies

*Ideal cookie jar filler-upper for after school or after work snacks.*

| | |
|---|---|
| Rolled oats | 3 cups |
| All-purpose flour | 2 1/2 cups |
| Baking soda | 1 1/2 tsp. |
| Cinnamon | 1 tsp. |
| Allspice | 1/2 tsp. |
| Salt | 1/2 tsp. |
| Raisins | 1 cup |
| Chopped walnuts | 1 cup |
| Currants | 1/2 cup |
| Coconut | 1/2 cup |
| Large eggs | 3 |
| Granulated sugar | 1 1/2 cups |
| Sour cream | 2 cups |
| Vanilla | 1 tsp. |

Measure first 10 ingredients into large bowl. Mix well.

In second bowl, beat eggs until frothy. Add sugar, sour cream and vanilla. Pour into dry ingredients in first bowl. Mix well. Drop by spoonfuls onto greased cookie sheet. Bake in 350°F oven for 10 to 15 minutes. Makes 8 dozen.

Pictured on page 71.

### Paré Pointer

*Two little birds were sent home from school. They were caught peeping during an exam.*

# Banana Drops

*These are great with or without cinnamon.*

| | |
|---|---|
| Butter (or hard margarine), softened | 1/2 cup |
| Granulated sugar | 1 cup |
| Large eggs | 2 |
| Mashed banana | 1 cup |
| All-purpose flour | 2 cups |
| Baking powder | 1 tbsp. |
| Salt | 1/4 tsp. |
| Chopped nuts | 1/2 cup |
| Raisins (optional) | 1 cup |
| Cinnamon (optional) | 1 tsp. |

Cream butter and sugar together. Beat in eggs 1 at a time. Add banana.

Measure in remaining ingredients. Mix well. Drop by spoonfuls onto greased cookie sheet. Bake in 375°F oven for 8 to 10 minutes. Makes 4 dozen.

Pictured on page 71.

Drop Cookies

# Orange Oat Crisps

*The grated orange rind gives these their distinctive flavor.*

| | |
|---|---|
| Large eggs | 2 |
| Granulated sugar | 1 cup |
| Brown sugar, packed | 1/2 cup |
| Cooking oil | 1 cup |
| All-purpose flour | 2 cups |
| Baking powder | 1 tsp. |
| Baking soda | 1/2 tsp. |
| Salt | 1/2 tsp. |
| Cinnamon | 1 tsp. |
| Grated orange rind | 1 tbsp. |
| Prepared orange juice (or milk) | 2 tbsp. |
| Rolled oats | 3 cups |

Beat eggs in mixing bowl until frothy. Beat in both sugars. Add cooking oil.

Stir next 5 ingredients together and add.

Add remaining ingredients. Mix well. Drop by spoonfuls onto greased cookie sheet. Bake in 350°F oven for 10 to 12 minutes. Makes about 5 dozen.

Pictured on page 71.

---

### Paré Pointer
*Eve knew she wouldn't get the mumps because she'd Adam.*

# Raisin Bran Cookies

*This could even be a breakfast cookie.*

| | |
|---|---|
| Butter (or hard margarine), softened | 1/2 cup |
| Brown sugar, packed | 1 cup |
| Large egg | 1 |
| Vanilla | 1 tsp. |
| All-purpose flour | 1 cup |
| Baking powder | 1 tsp. |
| Cinnamon (optional) | 1 tsp. |
| Salt | 1/2 tsp. |
| Raisins (optional) | 1/3 cup |
| Chopped nuts | 1/3 cup |
| All bran cereal | 1/2 cup |

Cream butter and sugar well. Beat in egg and vanilla.

Add remaining ingredients. Mix well. Drop by spoonfuls onto greased baking sheet. Flatten with wet fork. Bake in 350°F oven for 10 to 12 minutes. Makes 3 dozen.

Pictured on page 53.

# Chocolate Hermits

*A favorite cookie with an irresistible chocolate flavor.*

| | |
|---|---|
| Unsweetened chocolate squares | 6 × 1 oz. |
| Butter (or hard margarine), softened | 1 cup |
| Granulated sugar | 1 cup |
| Brown sugar, packed | 1 cup |
| Large eggs | 2 |
| Milk | 1/4 cup |
| Vanilla | 2 tsp. |
| All-purpose flour | 2 3/4 cups |
| Baking powder | 1 tbsp. |
| Baking soda | 1 tsp. |
| Cinnamon | 2 tsp. |
| Raisins | 1 1/2 cups |
| Chopped dates (optional) | 3/4 cup |
| Chopped nuts | 1 1/4 cups |

*(continued on next page)*

In small heavy saucepan melt chocolate over low heat. Set aside.

Cream butter and both sugars in mixing bowl. Beat in eggs 1 at a time. Add milk and vanilla. Stir. Add melted chocolate and mix well.

Stir flour, baking powder, baking soda and cinnamon together. Add to chocolate mixture. Mix well. Add raisins, dates and nuts. Stir. Drop by spoonfuls onto greased baking sheet. Bake in 350°F oven for about 13 to 15 minutes. If these flatten too much during baking, chill cookies before placing in oven. Makes 4 dozen.

Pictured on page 35.

# Quick Oatmeal Cookies

*An easy way to make oatmeal cookies. Try these with date filling as well.*

| | |
|---|---|
| **Rolled oats** | 3 cups |
| **Brown sugar, packed** | 1 cup |
| **All-purpose flour** | 1 cup |
| **Salt** | 1/2 tsp. |
| **Vanilla** | 1 tsp. |
| **Butter (or hard margarine), melted** | 1 cup |
| **Boiling water** | 1/4 cup |
| **Baking soda** | 1 tsp. |

Measure first 6 ingredients into mixing bowl. Mix together well.

Stir water and baking soda together. Add. Mix well. Shape into 2 inch rolls. Wrap and chill. Dough may also be frozen. When ready to bake slice thinly. Place on ungreased pan. Bake in 375°F oven for 8 to 10 minutes. Makes 4 dozen.

**QUICK DATE FILLED COOKIES:** Use Date Filling, page 94, to sandwich these cookies together. Saves rolling the dough. Excellent.

Pictured on pages 89 and 125.

# Shortbread

*So delicate! Keep a supply in the freezer. It thaws quickly.*

| | |
|---|---|
| Butter (not hard margarine), softened | 1 lb. |
| Sugar, use half brown and half icing (confectioner's) | 3/4 cup |
| All-purpose flour | 4 cups |

Red and green sugar, mixed
Candied cherries, cut up

Mix butter, sugar and flour together well. With your hands, squeeze and work until it will hold together. Make 4 rolls about 1 1/2 inches in diameter. May be sliced and baked at this point but makes a much rounder cookie if chilled first. May be chilled overnight or just an hour or two. Slice 1/4 inch thick. Arrange on ungreased baking sheet.

Sprinkle some cookies with sugar. Lightly push piece of cherry into center of some others. Bake in 325°F oven for about 15 to 20 minutes or until lightly browned around edges. Remove from baking sheet to counter top. Makes about 6 dozen.

**Note:** For a whiter shortbread use all icing sugar instead of part brown sugar. May also be rolled on lightly floured surface and cut into shapes.

Pictured on page 17.

# Ice Box Bran Cookies

*Crunchy good. Keep dough in refrigerator or freezer.*

| | |
|---|---|
| Butter (or hard margarine), softened | 1 1/2 cups |
| Brown sugar, packed | 2 cups |
| Large eggs | 2 |
| All-purpose flour | 3 cups |
| All bran cereal | 1 cup |
| Baking powder | 2 tsp. |

Cream butter and sugar together. Beat in eggs 1 at a time.

Stir in flour, cereal and baking powder. Shape into 2 inch rolls. Wrap and chill overnight. Next day slice thinly and arrange on ungreased baking sheet. Any unused dough may be frozen. Bake in 400°F oven for about 8 minutes. Makes 6 dozen.

Pictured on page 89.

**58**

# Christmas Ice Box Cookies

*Good any other time as well. Pretty on a plate of goodies.*

| | |
|---|---|
| Butter (or hard margarine), softened | 1 cup |
| Brown sugar, packed | 1 1/2 cups |
| Large eggs | 2 |
| Vanilla | 1 tsp. |
| All-purpose flour | 3 1/2 cups |
| Baking soda | 1 tsp. |
| Salt | 1/4 tsp. |
| Candied cherries, quartered | 3/4 cup |
| Finely chopped nuts | 1/2 cup |
| Currants (optional) | 1/2 cup |

In mixing bowl cream butter and sugar together. Beat eggs in 1 at a time. Add vanilla.

Stir flour, baking soda and salt together and mix in. Add cherries, nuts and currants. Mix and shape into round or square logs approximately 2 inches in diameter. Wrap and chill overnight or longer. May be frozen also. When ready to bake slice thinly. Arrange on ungreased baking sheet. Bake in 375°F oven for 6 to 7 minutes until very light brown.

Pictured on page 17.

# Cream Cheese Cookies

*These little rounds are topped with jam and baked. Some are rolled.*

| | |
|---|---|
| Butter (or hard margarine), softened | 1/2 cup |
| Cream cheese, softened | 2 oz. |
| Granulated sugar | 1/3 cup |
| Vanilla | 1/2 tsp. |
| All-purpose flour | 1 cup |
| Jam, red or orange | |

Mix first five ingredients together. Shape into 2 logs, 1 1/2 inches in diameter. Wrap and chill overnight. Dough may be frozen.

When ready to bake, slice into 1/4 inch slices. Put dab of jam on each. Place on ungreased baking sheet. Bake in 350°F oven for about 10 minutes until golden brown. Makes 3 dozen.

**CRESCENT-ROLL CREAM CHEESE COOKIES:** Instead of slicing the logs, roll out 1/4 inch thick and cut into 2 inch squares. Put dab of jam in center of each. Roll up, starting at corner and shape like crescent. Bake as above.

Pictured on page 16.

# Chocolate Ice Box Cookies

*Dark and delicious. For a solid chocolate appearance, simply omit the nuts or roll logs in nuts before chilling.*

| | |
|---|---|
| Butter (or hard margarine), softened | 3/4 cup |
| Granulated sugar | 1 cup |
| Large egg | 1 |
| Vanilla | 1 tsp. |
| Unsweetened chocolate squares, melted | 3 x 1 oz. |
| All-purpose flour | 2 1/2 cups |
| Baking powder | 1 1/2 tsp. |
| Salt | 1/2 tsp. |
| Finely chopped pecans or walnuts | 1 cup |

Cream butter and sugar together. Beat in egg, vanilla and melted chocolate.

Add remaining ingredients. Mix together. Shape into rolls 2 inches in diameter or oblongs 1 x 2 inches. Wrap in waxed paper or plastic. Chill overnight or longer. May also be frozen. To bake, slice thinly and place on ungreased cookie sheet. Bake in 375°F oven for about 5 minutes. Makes 8 to 9 dozen.

Pictured on page 17.

# Vanilla Wafers

*For variety, add 1 tbsp. powdered instant coffee granules to make coffee wafers.*

| | |
|---|---|
| Butter (or hard margarine), softened | 1/2 cup |
| Granulated sugar | 3/4 cup |
| Large egg | 1 |
| Corn syrup | 2 tbsp. |
| Vanilla | 1 tsp. |
| Baking soda | 2 tsp. |
| Hot water | 1 tbsp. |
| All-purpose flour | 2 1/3 cups |

Cream butter and sugar together. Beat in egg, syrup, and vanilla.

Dissolve baking soda in water. Add.

Mix in flour. Shape into 2 inch rolls. Wrap and chill overnight or longer. Slice thinly and place on ungreased cookie sheet. Bake in 400°F oven for 6 to 8 minutes. Makes about 8 dozen.

Pictured on page 125.

Ice Box Cookies

# Spiced Ice Box Cookies

*These are spicy, crisp and good keepers.*

| | |
|---|---|
| Butter (or hard margarine), softened | 1 cup |
| Brown sugar, packed | 2/3 cup |
| Granulated sugar | 2/3 cup |
| Large eggs | 2 |
| Vanilla | 1 tsp. |
| All-purpose flour | 3 cups |
| Baking soda | 1 tsp. |
| Salt | 1/2 tsp. |
| Cinnamon | 1 tsp. |
| Nutmeg | 1/4 tsp. |
| Cloves | 1/4 tsp. |
| Chopped nuts | 1/2 cup |

Cream butter and both sugars together well. Beat in eggs and vanilla.

Stir remaining ingredients together and add. Mix well. Roll into 2 inch square or round logs. Wrap and chill overnight. Dough may also be frozen. When ready to bake slice thinly. Place on ungreased baking sheet. Bake in 375°F oven for about 8 minutes. Makes 4 1/2 to 5 dozen.

Pictured on page 89.

# Ice Box Mincemeat Cookies

*These spicy cookies are a bit softer than most ice box varieties.*

| | |
|---|---|
| Butter (or hard margarine), softened | 1 cup |
| Brown sugar, packed | 1 cup |
| Large egg | 1 |
| Mincemeat | 1 cup |
| All-purpose flour | 3 cups |
| Baking soda | 1 tsp. |
| Salt | 1/2 tsp. |

Cream butter and sugar together. Beat in egg. Add mincemeat.

Stir flour, baking soda and salt together and add. Mix well. Shape into rolls 2 inches in diameter. Wrap and chill overnight. When ready to bake slice thinly and arrange on greased baking sheet. Bake in 400°F oven for 6 to 8 minutes. Makes 5 dozen.

Pictured on page 53.

# Date Pinwheels

*Another old favorite. Make one day and bake the next.*

| FILLING | |
| --- | --- |
| Dates, chopped | 1 lb. |
| Granulated sugar | 1/2 cup |
| Water | 1/3 cup |
| Finely chopped walnuts | 2/3 cup |
| COOKIE DOUGH | |
| Butter (or hard margarine), softened | 1 cup |
| Brown sugar, packed | 1 cup |
| Granulated sugar | 1 cup |
| Large eggs | 2 |
| Vanilla | 2 tsp. |
| All-purpose flour | 3 1/2 cups |
| Baking soda | 1 tsp. |
| Salt | 1/2 tsp. |

**Filling:** Simmer dates, sugar and water together until mushy and thickened. Add a bit more water if too dry.

Stir in nuts. Cool.

**Cookie Dough:** Cream butter with sugars in mixing bowl. Beat in eggs 1 at a time. Add vanilla.

Stir in flour, baking soda and salt. Divide dough into 4 parts. Roll each part 1/4 inch thick, in rectangular shape. Spread with date filling. Roll. Chill overnight. Slice 1/4 inch thick. Place on greased cookie sheet. Bake in 375°F oven for 8 to 10 minutes. Makes about 8 dozen.

Pictured on page 143.

**RASPBERRY PINWHEELS:** Omit date mixture. Spread dough with a mixture of 1 cup raspberry jam, 1 cup shredded coconut and 1/2 cup finely chopped nuts. Makes 8 dozen.

**CHOCOLATE PINWHEELS:** Spread 1/4 dough with 1/2 cup semisweet chocolate chips, melted. Roll, wrap and chill. Bring to room temperature before slicing otherwise chocolate is too hard. These are delicious.

Pictured on page 53.

Ice Box Cookies

# Cherry Ice Box Cookies

*A pretty cookie speckled with bits of red cherries.*

| | |
|---|---|
| Butter (not margarine), softened | 1 cup |
| Brown sugar, packed | 2/3 cup |
| Large eggs | 2 |
| Almond flavoring | 1 tsp. |
| All-purpose flour | 2 1/2 cups |
| Candied cherries, cut up | 1 cup |
| Finely chopped almonds | 1/2 cup |

Cream butter and sugar together well. Beat in eggs and almond flavoring.

Add flour, cherries and almonds. Work into dough. Form into rolls 1 1/2 inches or so in diameter. Wrap in waxed paper or plastic. Chill overnight or longer. May also be frozen. To bake, slice thinly and place on greased baking sheet. Bake in 375°F oven for 6 to 8 minutes. Makes about 7 dozen.

Pictured on page 89.

# Santa's Whiskers

*Make these one day and bake the next. A colorful cookie.*

| | |
|---|---|
| Butter (or hard margarine), softened | 1 cup |
| Granulated sugar | 1 cup |
| Vanilla | 1 tsp. |
| Milk | 2 tbsp. |
| All-purpose flour | 2 1/2 cups |
| Finely chopped candied cherries, red and green | 3/4 cup |
| Chopped pecans | 1/2 cup |
| Flaked coconut | 1 cup |

Mix first 7 ingredients together well. Shape into 2 rolls 2 inches in diameter. Add a bit more milk if too dry to hold together.

Roll in coconut. Cover and chill overnight. Next day slice 1/4 inch thick. Arrange on ungreased cookie sheet. Bake in 375°F oven for about 10 to 12 minutes or until edges are lightly browned. Makes 4 to 5 dozen.

Pictured on page 17.

# Shortbread Pinwheels

*Make one day and bake the next. The rolls of white and chocolate make an interesting design. By omitting cocoa and tinting one half of the dough pink you will have a delicately colored pinwheel.*

| | |
|---|---|
| Butter (not margarine), softened | 1 cup |
| Icing (confectioner's) sugar | 2/3 cup |
| Vanilla | 1/2 tsp. |
| All-purpose flour | 2 cups |
| Cocoa | 1/4 cup |

Cream butter and sugar together. Mix in vanilla and flour. Divide dough into 2 equal portions.

To.1 portion add cocoa. Mix well. Roll chocolate portion between 2 layers of waxed paper. Roll to a size of 7 1/2 × 12 inches. Remove top waxed paper. Roll white dough portion between 2 layers of waxed paper. Roll to a size of 7 × 12 inches. Remove top paper. Invert over chocolate layer keeping ends together at 1 end. Chocolate layer will extend a bit at the other end. Remove top paper. Roll from short end with edges even removing bottom paper as you roll. When rolled, complete outside edge will be chocolate. Wrap and chill overnight or longer. When ready to bake slice 1/3 inch thick. Arrange on ungreased baking sheet. Bake in 350°F oven for 10 to 12 minutes. Makes about 26 cookies.

Pictured on pages 89, 143 and on cover.

**CLOVERLEAF:** Omit cocoa. Divide dough into 3 portions, tint 1 yellow, 1 pink, 1 green as shown on page 116. Chill.

**CHECKERBOARD:** Make 4 ropes, 2 white and 2 chocolate as shown on page 116. Chill.

# Pinwheels

*Dark and light stripes in a striking design. Dough may be frozen.*

| | |
|---|---|
| Butter (or hard margarine), softened | 1/2 cup |
| Granulated sugar | 1/2 cup |
| Large egg | 1 |
| Vanilla | 1 tsp. |
| Milk | 3 tbsp. |
| All-purpose flour | 1 3/4 cups |
| Baking powder | 1/2 tsp. |
| Salt | 1/8 tsp. |

*(continued on next page)*

| Cocoa | 2 tbsp. |
| Butter (or hard margarine), softened | 1 tbsp. |

Cream first amount of butter and sugar together. Beat in egg, vanilla and milk.

Stir flour, baking powder and salt together and add. Mix into a ball. Divide into 2 equal portions.

To 1 portion add cocoa and remaining butter. Mix well. Roll out each portion between sheets of waxed paper to 1/8 inch thick. Make them the same size in a rectangular shape. Remove top papers. Invert white layer over chocolate. Remove top paper. Roll as for jelly roll, removing bottom paper as you roll. Wrap and chill overnight. To bake slice thinly. Place on ungreased cookie sheet. Bake in 375°F oven for about 6 minutes. Makes 4 dozen.

Pictured on page 143.

# Peanut Butter Ice Box Cookies

*Make your cookie dough ahead to have on hand.*

| Butter (or hard margarine), softened | 1/2 cup |
| Smooth peanut butter | 1/2 cup |
| Brown sugar, packed | 1 cup |
| Large eggs | 2 |
| Vanilla | 1 tsp. |
| All-purpose flour | 2 1/2 cups |
| Baking powder | 1 tsp. |
| Salt | 1 tsp. |

In bowl cream butter, peanut butter and sugar. Beat in eggs 1 at a time. Add vanilla.

Reserve 1/4 cup flour. Stir rest of flour, baking powder and salt together and mix in. Work in as much reserved flour as you can. Shape into 3 rolls 2 inches in diameter. Wrap and chill overnight or longer. When ready to bake slice thinly. Place on ungreased sheet. Bake in 375°F oven for 6 to 8 minutes. Makes 5 dozen.

**CHOCOLATE GLAZE**

| Semi-sweet chocolate squares | 3 x 1 oz. |
| Grated parowax (paraffin) | 2 tbsp. |

Melt chocolate and parowax together over low heat. Dip corner of cookies. Dry on waxed paper.

Pictured on page 125.

# Lemon Ice Box Cookies

*Crisp and lemony. Add glaze to give an extra touch.*

| | |
|---|---|
| Butter (or hard margarine), softened | 1 cup |
| Granulated sugar | 3/4 cup |
| Large eggs | 2 |
| Grated lemon rind | 1 tbsp. |
| All-purpose flour | 3 cups |
| Baking powder | 1/2 tsp. |
| Salt | 1/4 tsp. |

Cream butter and sugar together well. Beat in eggs, 1 at a time. Add lemon rind.

Stir flour, baking powder and salt together and mix in. Shape into rolls about 2 inches in diameter. Wrap and chill overnight. Dough may also be frozen. Next day slice thinly and place on ungreased cookie sheets. Bake in 375°F oven for 7 to 10 minutes. Makes about 5 dozen.

**GLAZE:** Mix 1/2 cup icing (confectioner's) sugar with enough lemon juice to make a barely pourable glaze. Add yellow food coloring if desired. Spread on cookies.

Pictured on page 125.

# Ice Box Ginger Cookies

*These crisp cookies keep well. A popular flavor.*

| | |
|---|---|
| Butter (or hard margarine), softened | 1 cup |
| Granulated sugar | 1 1/2 cups |
| Large egg | 1 |
| Corn syrup | 2 tbsp. |
| Baking soda | 2 tsp. |
| Warm water | 1 tbsp. |
| Grated rind of large whole orange | 1 |
| All-purpose flour | 3 cups |
| Ginger | 2 tsp. |
| Cinnamon | 2 tsp. |
| Cloves | 1/2 tsp. |

*(continued on next page)*

Cream butter and sugar together. Beat in egg and corn syrup.

Dissolve baking soda in water and mix in.

Stir in remaining ingredients. Mix well. Shape into 2 inch rolls. Wrap and chill overnight or longer. Dough may be frozen. When ready to bake, slice thinly. Place on ungreased baking sheet. Bake in 400°F oven for 8 to 10 minutes. Makes 6 dozen, 3 inch cookies.

Pictured on page 53.

# Butterscotch Cookies

*A favorite flavor for everybody. Crisp.*

| | |
|---|---|
| Butter (or hard margarine), softened | 1 cup |
| Brown sugar, packed | 2 cups |
| Large eggs | 2 |
| Vanilla | 1 tsp. |
| Chopped walnuts | 1 cup |
| All-purpose flour | 3 cups |
| Baking soda | 1 tsp. |

Cream butter and sugar together in mixing bowl. Beat in eggs 1 at a time. Stir in vanilla and nuts.

Stir flour and baking soda together and add to mixture. Shape into rolls about 2 inches in diameter. Wrap in waxed paper or plastic and chill overnight or longer. When ready to bake, slice however many you want and freeze the rest of the dough. To bake, slice thinly and arrange on ungreased cookie sheet. Bake in 350°F oven for about 8 to 10 minutes. Makes about 12 dozen.

Pictured on page 71.

## Paré Pointer
*The best thing for nail biting is sharp teeth.*

# Ice Box Ribbons

*Three pretty layers baked as one cookie. Freezes well before or after baking.*

| | |
|---|---|
| Butter (or hard margarine), softened | 1 cup |
| Granulated sugar | 1 cup |
| Large egg | 1 |
| Vanilla | 1 tsp. |
| | |
| All-purpose flour | 2 1/2 cups |
| Baking powder | 1 tsp. |
| Salt | 1/4 tsp. |
| | |
| Red food coloring | |
| Chopped candied red cherries | 1/4 cup |
| | |
| Semisweet chocolate chips, melted | 1/3 cup |
| Chopped nuts | 1/3 cup |
| | |
| Coconut | 1/3 cup |

Cream butter and sugar together. Beat in egg and vanilla.

Stir flour, baking powder and salt together and mix in. Divide dough into 3 equal parts.

**First Layer:** To 1 part of dough mix in enough red food coloring to tint a pretty pink. Add cherries. Combine and pack into 8 x 4 inch foil-lined loaf pan.

**Second Layer:** To second part of dough mix in chocolate and nuts. Pack evenly over first layer.

**Third Layer:** To last part of dough mix in coconut. Pack over second layer. Wrap and chill overnight. When ready to bake remove foil from dough. Cut into slices 1/4 inch thick. Then cut each slice into 3 pieces. Arrange on ungreased cookie sheet. Bake in 350°F oven for 10 to 12 minutes. Makes about 5 1/2 dozen.

Pictured on page 17.

## Paré Pointer

*With an earthquake and a forest fire you have shake and bake.*

# Peanut Butter Cups

*A real treat for any age. Takes extra time to dip in chocolate.*

| | |
|---|---|
| Smooth peanut butter | 1 1/2 cups |
| Butter (or hard margarine), softened | 1/4 cup |
| Icing (confectioner's) sugar | 2 cups |
| Vanilla | 1 tsp. |
| | |
| Semisweet chocolate chips | 2 cups |
| Grated parowax (paraffin) | 1/3 cup |

Mix first 4 ingredients together. Shape into 1 inch balls. May be shaped into logs as well using same amount of dough.

Melt chocolate chips and wax in small heavy saucepan over low heat. Dip balls, drain and place on waxed paper. Makes about 7 1/2 dozen.

Pictured on page 17.

# Creamy Snowballs

*If you have a sweet tooth these are for you. Creamy.*

| | |
|---|---|
| Cream cheese, softened | 4 oz. |
| Icing (confectioner's) sugar | 2 cups |
| Milk | 2 tbsp. |
| Semisweet chocolate chips, melted | 2/3 cup |
| Vanilla | 1/2 tsp. |
| | |
| Miniature colored marshmallows | 3 cups |
| | |
| Coconut | |

Combine first 5 ingredients together in bowl. Beat together until smooth.

Fold in marshmallows. Mix well. Chill for 30 minutes. Shape into 1 1/2 inch balls.

Roll in coconut. These freeze well. Makes about 3 1/2 dozen.

Pictured on page 17.

# Date Coconut Balls

*With these in the freezer you will always have a party-type cookie*
*on hand. Made in a saucepan.*

| | |
|---|---|
| Chopped dates | 1 1/2 cups |
| Brown sugar, packed | 1 cup |
| Butter (or hard margarine) | 1 tbsp. |
| Large eggs | 2 |
| Vanilla | 1 tsp. |
| Crisp rice cereal | 2 cups |
| Finely chopped nuts | 1/2 cup |
| Finely chopped cherries | 1/4 cup |
| Shredded coconut | |

Combine dates, sugar, butter, eggs and vanilla in saucepan. Heat. Cook, stirring constantly, for about 5 minutes.

Stir in cereal, nuts and cherries. Cool until mixture is warm. Shape into 1 inch balls.

Roll balls in coconut. Butter hands to prevent dough from sticking. Makes 4 dozen.

Pictured on page 143.

1.  Spicy Dads, page 34
2.  Crackerjack Cookies, page 117
3.  Ginger Snaps, page 111
4.  Brown Sugar Cookies, page 29
5.  Cornmeal Crisps, page 101
6.  Cornflake Cookies, page 11
7.  Pop's Cookies, page 132
8.  Chocolate Peanut Drops, page 84
9.  Raisin Nut Drops, page 15
10. Banana Drops, page 52
11. War-Time Cookies, page 117
12. Potato Chip Cookies, page 128
13. Brown Sugar Cookies, page 29
14. Butterscotch Cookies, page 67
15. Best Drop Cookies, page 25
16. Oatmeal Chip Cookies, page 27
17. Coconut Crumb Cookies, page 28
18. Orange Oat Crisps, page 55
19. Peanut Molasses Cookies, page 12
20. Pumpkin Cookies, page 10
21. Pop's Cookies, page 132
22. Orange Coconut Cookies, page 10
23. Pumpkin Cookies with raisins, page 10
24. Thresher's Cookies, page 51
25. Oatmeal Cookies, page 39
26. Pumpkin Cookies with chocolate chips, page 10
27. Oatmeal Chip Cookies, page 27

No Bake Cookies

# Coconut Logs

*Like your favorite coconut chocolate bar. No baking.*

| | |
|---|---|
| Icing (confectioner's) sugar | 2 cups |
| Flaked coconut | 2 cups |
| Milk | 2 tbsp. |
| Butter (or hard margarine), softened | 1 tbsp. |
| Semisweet chocolate chips | 1 cup |
| Grated parowax (paraffin) | 3 tbsp. |

Mix first 4 ingredients together well. Shape into thumb size logs.

Melt chocolate chips and parowax in small saucepan over low heat. Dip logs in chocolate to cover. Drain and place on waxed paper. Makes 2 1/2 dozen.

Pictured on page 17.

# Ginger Choco Cookies

*These no bake cookies are made from ginger snap crumbs.*
*They are soft and creamy.*

| | |
|---|---|
| Semisweet chocolate chips | 2 cups |
| Sour cream | 1/2 cup |
| Lemon juice | 1 tsp. |
| Ginger snap crumbs | 2 cups |
| Icing (confectioner's) sugar | 1 cup |

Melt chocolate chips in sour cream and lemon juice in medium size, heavy saucepan over low heat. Stir often to hasten melting. Be careful not to boil. Remove from heat.

Add cookie crumbs and icing sugar. Stir to moisten. Shape into 1 inch balls. These may be left as is or rolled in icing sugar or dipped in chocolate glaze. Makes about 6 dozen.

**CHOCOLATE GLAZE:** Mix 1 cup icing (confectioner's) sugar with 2 tbsp. cocoa. Add enough water to make a barely pourable glaze. Dip tops of cookie balls and leave to dry on tray.

Pictured on page 107.

# Chocolate Crisps

*No oven to make these chocolaty good drops.*

| | |
|---|---|
| Semisweet chocolate chips | 2 cups |
| Crisp rice cereal | 2 cups |
| Shredded coconut | 1 cup |

Melt chips in heavy saucepan over low heat.

Mix in cereal and coconut. Drop by spoonfuls onto waxed paper. Let harden. Makes 3 dozen.

Pictured on page 125.

# Boiled Chocolate Cookies

*This is probably the most used recipe of young first-time cooks.*
*No oven required.*

| | |
|---|---|
| Butter (or hard margarine) | 1/2 cup |
| Milk | 1/2 cup |
| Granulated sugar | 2 cups |
| Cocoa | 1/2 cup |
| Rolled oats | 2 1/2 cups |

Put butter, milk, sugar and cocoa into saucepan. Bring to a boil stirring often. Boil 5 minutes.

Remove from heat. Stir in rolled oats. Drop by teaspoonfuls onto waxed paper. Makes about 4 dozen.

**Variation:** To make these more special, coconut, cherries and/or nuts may be added.

Pictured on page 89.

### *Paré Pointer*
*A rug you take up and shake and medicine you shake up and take.*

No Bake Cookies

# Peanut Butter Drops

*A splendid variation of a boiled chocolate cookie.*

| | |
|---|---|
| Butter (or hard margarine) | 1/2 cup |
| Milk | 1/2 cup |
| Granulated sugar | 1 3/4 cups |
| Cocoa | 1/2 cup |
| Rolled oats | 3 cups |
| Smooth peanut butter | 1/2 cup |

Measure first 4 ingredients into medium saucepan. Bring to a boil over medium heat stirring often. Boil for 3 minutes. Remove from heat.

Add rolled oats and peanut butter. Mix well. Drop by spoonfuls onto waxed paper. Freezes. Makes about 5 dozen.

Pictured on page 107.

# Cracker Snack

*From crackers come these peanut butter cookies. Dipped in chocolate, they become an extra special treat. No baking.*

| | |
|---|---|
| Round mild flavored crackers | 48 |
| Smooth peanut butter | 1 cup |
| Semisweet chocolate squares | 8 x 1 oz. |
| Grated parowax (paraffin) | 1/4 cup |

Spread crackers liberally with peanut butter, making sandwich style. It is not necessary to use the amount given.

Melt chocolate with wax over hot water. Dip sandwiched crackers, then place on waxed paper. Makes 2 dozen.

**PRETZEL SNACK:** Dip pretzels in chocolate-wax mixture. A quick treat.

Pictured on page 107.

# Cream Cheese Balls

*These creamy cookies need no baking. The addition of cherries gives them color.*

| | |
|---|---|
| Cream cheese, softened | 8 oz. |
| Icing (confectioner's) sugar | 1 cup |
| Coconut | 1 cup |
| Maraschino cherries, finely chopped | 15 |
| Crushed pineapple, drained | 14 oz. |
| Vanilla wafer crumbs | 3 cups |
| COATING | |
| Butter (or hard margarine) | 2 tbsp. |
| Granulated sugar | 1 tbsp. |
| Graham cracker crumbs | 3/4 cup |

Beat cream cheese and icing sugar together. Mix in coconut and cherries. Stir in pineapple and crumbs. Chill for 30 minutes. Shape into 1 inch balls.

**Coating:** Melt butter in small saucepan. Remove from heat. Stir in sugar and crumbs. Roll cookies in this mixture. Freezes well. Makes about 5 dozen.

Pictured on page 53.

# Noodle Power

*These little stacks are shiny and ever so good. They are softer and easier to bite into than other similar cookies.*

| | |
|---|---|
| Semisweet chocolate chips | 1 cup |
| Butterscotch chips | 1 cup |
| Butter (or hard margarine) | 1/4 cup |
| Smooth peanut butter | 1/4 cup |
| Peanuts | 1 cup |
| Dry Chinese noodles | 2 cups |

Melt first 4 ingredients in large saucepan over low heat. Stir often. Remove from heat.

Mix in peanuts and noodles. Spoon into mounds on waxed paper. Mixture will seem soft but it will firm upon standing. May be chilled to hasten hardening. Makes 2 1/2 dozen.

Pictured on page 125.

**76**

# Coconut Peaks

*Chocolate peaks take the spotlight when these are served. A no bake treat.*

| | |
|---|---|
| Butter (or hard margarine) | 1/4 cup |
| Icing (confectioner's) sugar | 2 cups |
| Light cream | 2 tbsp. |
| Flaked coconut | 3 cups |
| | |
| Semisweet chocolate chips | 1 cup |
| Butter (or hard margarine) | 1 tbsp. |

Melt first amount of butter in saucepan. Remove from heat. Stir in icing sugar, cream and coconut. Shape into small balls, then squeeze top to form peaks which resemble tiny haystacks. Place on tray. Put in refrigerator, uncovered. Let dry overnight.

In small saucepan, over low heat, melt chocolate chips and remaining butter together. Stir often. Dip tops of peaks. Freezes well. Makes 2 1/2 dozen.

Pictured on page 17.

# Peanut Butter Balls

*These crispy-crunch balls are the best! Fabulous. My favorite.*

| | |
|---|---|
| Smooth peanut butter | 1 cup |
| Icing (confectioner's) sugar | 1 cup |
| Crisp rice cereal | 1 cup |
| Finely chopped walnuts | 1/2 cup |
| Butter (or hard margarine), softened | 1 tbsp. |
| | |
| Semisweet chocolate squares | 4 x 1 oz. |
| Grated parowax (paraffin) | 2 tbsp. |

Measure first 5 ingredients into bowl. With your hands, mix together well. Shape into 1 inch balls. Chill for 2 to 3 hours.

Melt chocolate chips and wax together. Dip balls to coat, drain and place on waxed paper. Makes 4 1/2 to 5 dozen.

Pictured on page 125.

# Glazed Coffee Balls

*Not even a saucepan is needed for these little morsels. Just mix,*
*shape, then dip in coffee flavored glaze.*

| | |
|---|---|
| Graham cracker crumbs | 2 cups |
| Icing (confectioner's) sugar | 1/2 cup |
| Finely chopped pecans | 1/2 cup |
| Hot water | 1/2 cup |
| Instant coffee granules | 1 tsp. |
| Butter (or hard margarine) | 2 tbsp. |
| GLAZE | |
| Icing (confectioner's) sugar | 1 cup |
| Butter (or hard margarine), softened | 1 tbsp. |
| Prepared coffee | 1 tbsp. |

Measure crumbs, icing sugar and pecans into bowl.

In measuring cup measure hot water. Stir in coffee granules and butter to melt. Pour over crumb mixture. Stir well. Form into small balls. Dip in glaze.

**Glaze:** Mix sugar, butter and coffee, adding more sugar or coffee if needed for proper consistency. Dip balls in glaze. Let dry on waxed paper. Makes about 40.

Pictured on page 125.

# Coconut Fruit Bites

*These tangy little balls have no sugar added. No baking. Just mix and shape.*

| | |
|---|---|
| Dates, cut up | 1 cup |
| Dried apricots, cut up | 1 cup |
| Raisins | 1 cup |
| Chopped walnuts | 1 cup |
| Coconut | 1 cup |
| Coconut | |

Grind dates, apricots and raisins or use food processor.

Add nuts and first amount of coconut. Shape into 1 inch balls.

Roll in coconut. Freezes well. Makes about 4 dozen.

Pictured on page 89.

**78**  No Bake Cookies

# Choco Coconut Balls

*These dark colored balls have white centers. No oven needed.*

| | |
|---|---|
| Butter (or hard margarine) | 1/4 cup |
| Sweetened condensed milk | 2/3 cup |
| Icing (confectioner's) sugar | 3 1/3 cups |
| Coconut | 1/2 cup |
| Chopped pecans or walnuts | 1 cup |
| Semisweet chocolate chips | 1 cup |
| Grated parowax (paraffin) | 3 tbsp. |

Melt butter in saucepan. Stir in milk and sugar. Remove from heat.

Add coconut and nuts. Add more icing sugar if it seems too soft. Chill. Roll into 1 inch balls.

Melt chocolate chips and wax in small saucepan over low heat. Dip balls to coat. Drain and place on waxed paper. Makes about 6 dozen.

Pictured on page 125.

# Coconut Balls

*These are not too sweet. No baking.*

| | |
|---|---|
| Sweetened condensed milk | 14 oz. |
| Semisweet chocolate chips | 2/3 cup |
| Chopped nuts | 1/2 cup |
| Graham cracker crumbs | 2 1/2 cups |
| Coconut | |

In bowl mix first 4 ingredients together. Shape into 1 inch balls.

Roll in coconut. Makes 5 dozen.

Pictured on page 89.

# Peanut Butter Chip Balls

*Just a few ingredients for these. Dipping is optional.*

| | |
|---|---|
| Smooth peanut butter | 1 cup |
| Sweetened condensed milk | 1/2 cup |
| Icing (confectioner's) sugar | 1/2 cup |
| Semisweet chocolate chips | 1 cup |

Mix all ingredients together. Shape into balls. Place on waxed paper. Chill to set. Makes about 4 dozen.

**CHOCOLATE COATING:** Melt 1 cup semisweet chocolate chips and 3 tbsp. grated parowax (paraffin) in heavy saucepan or over hot water in double boiler. Dip balls and place on waxed paper to dry.

Pictured on page 125.

# Toffee Cookies

*These are ever so yummy. No baking required.*

| | |
|---|---|
| Caramels (about 36) | 8 oz. |
| Cream (light) | 3 tbsp. |
| Cornflakes | 2 cups |
| Crisp rice cereal | 1 cup |
| Coconut | 1/2 cup |

Put caramels and cream into large heavy saucepan over low heat to melt.

Add remaining ingredients. Stir to coat. Drop by spoonfuls onto greased surface. Leave to harden. Makes about 3 1/2 dozen.

Pictured on page 35.

## Paré Pointer
*All sick ponies go to the horse-pital.*

No Bake Cookies

# Peanut Butter Bites

*A snap to make. No baking for this grand cookie. Dip tops in melted chocolate chips and nuts for a festive look.*

| | |
|---|---|
| Smooth peanut butter | 1/2 cup |
| Icing (confectioner's) sugar | 1/2 cup |
| Graham cracker crumbs | 1/2 cup |

Finely chopped nuts, cocoa, icing sugar, chocolate sprinkles

Mix first 3 ingredients together. Shape into 1 inch balls.

Roll in nuts, cocoa, icing sugar or chocolate sprinkles. Freezes well. Makes about 3 dozen.

Pictured on page 89.

# Apricot Jam Balls

*Make these no bake cookies in a jiffy.*

| | |
|---|---|
| Apricot jam | 1/2 cup |
| Butter (or hard margarine) | 2 tbsp. |
| Graham cracker crumbs | 2 cups |
| Rum flavoring | 1/2 tsp. |

Medium coconut

Combine jam and butter in medium size saucepan. Heat and stir to boiling. Remove from heat.

Stir in graham crumbs and flavoring. Roll into 1 inch balls.

Roll in medium coconut. Makes 28.

Pictured on page 107.

### Paré Pointer
*Cinderella couldn't play football. Her coach was a pumpkin.*

# Butterscotch Noodles

*Make these in a saucepan. Quick and easy.*

| | |
|---|---|
| Butterscotch chips | 2 cups |
| Butter (or hard margarine) | 1/2 cup |
| Peanuts | 1 cup |
| Dry Chinese chow mein noodles | 2 cups |

Melt chips and butter in heavy saucepan over low heat. Stir to hasten melting. Stir in peanuts and noodles. Drop by spoonfuls onto waxed paper. Makes 3 dozen.

**PEANUT BUTTER NOODLES:** Add 2 tbsp. smooth peanut butter.

Pictured on page 107.

# Peanut Graham Morsels

*No need to bake these flavorful bites.*

| | |
|---|---|
| Butter (or hard margarine), softened | 1/2 cup |
| Smooth peanut butter | 3/4 cup |
| Coconut or chopped nuts | 1/2 cup |
| Icing (confectioner's) sugar | 1 3/4 cups |
| Graham cracker crumbs | 1 cup |
| Semisweet chocolate chips | 1 cup |
| Grated parowax (paraffin) | 3 tbsp. |

Mix first 5 ingredients together in bowl. Shape into 1 inch balls and logs using same amount of dough for logs.

Melt chocolate chips with parowax. Either dip to coat or just dip tops. Place on waxed paper. Makes 6 dozen.

Pictured on page 125.

### Paré Pointer
*Definition of a snake: a tail without a body.*

No Bake Cookies

# Creamy Morsels

*These good rich rolls begin in a saucepan followed by chilling. Roll into logs and then in coconut.*

| | |
|---|---|
| Semisweet chocolate chips | 1 cup |
| Butterscotch chips | 1 cup |
| Cream cheese, softened | 8 oz. |
| Candied cherries, quartered | 1 cup |
| Tiny marshmallows, halved | 2 1/2 cups |
| Coconut | |

Put chocolate and butterscotch chips in medium size saucepan over low heat. Melt, stirring often. Remove from heat.

Add cheese in small pieces. Stir in cherries and marshmallows. Chill until it starts to firm.

Shape into thumb size logs. Roll in coconut. Freezes. Makes about 5 dozen.

Pictured on page 107.

# Peanut Balls

*Chewy and much like toffee. Good peanut flavor. No baking needed.*

| | |
|---|---|
| Finely chopped peanuts | 3 cups |
| Sweetened condensed milk | 14 oz. |
| Ground peanuts to coat | |

Combine peanuts and milk in heavy saucepan. Heat and stir until boiling. Stir constantly for 5 minutes until mixture forms a ball and leaves sides of pan. Cool to room temperature. Shape into 1 inch balls.

Roll in ground peanuts. Makes about 4 1/2 dozen.

Pictured on page 89.

### Paré Pointer
*Billy eats with his knife because his fork leaks.*

No Bake Cookies

# Apricot Balls

*No cooking for this one. Not too sweet.*

| | |
|---|---|
| Ground dried apricots | 1/2 lb. |
| Medium coconut | 2 cups |
| Icing (confectioner's) sugar | 1/4 cup |
| Finely chopped nuts | 1/2 cup |
| Sweetened condensed milk | 1/2 cup |
| Grated orange rind | 1/2 tsp. |

Mix all ingredients together. Roll into 1 inch balls. Chill. Makes 5 dozen.

Pictured on page 53.

# Chocolate Peanut Drops

*Peanut butter adds to the flavor of these saucepan cookies.*

| | |
|---|---|
| Milk | 1/2 cup |
| Butter (or hard margarine) | 1/2 cup |
| Granulated sugar | 2 cups |
| Cocoa | 6 tbsp. |
| Smooth peanut butter | 3/4 cup |
| Vanilla | 1 tsp. |
| Rolled oats | 3 cups |
| Chopped nuts (optional) | 1/2 cup |

Put milk, butter, sugar and cocoa in medium size saucepan. Heat and stir until boiling. Remove from heat.

Stir in peanut butter and vanilla. Add rolled oats and nuts. Mix. Drop by spoonfuls onto waxed paper. Makes about 4 1/2 dozen.

Pictured on page 71.

### Paré Pointer

*All he talks about is his ancestors. His family is better dead than alive.*

No Bake Cookies

# Granola Stacks

*A tasty mixture of cereal and raisins combined with melted chips. No oven needed.*

| | |
|---|---|
| Semisweet chocolate chips | 1 cup |
| Butterscotch chips | 1 cup |
| Granola cereal | 1 1/4 cups |
| Raisins (optional) | 1/4 cup |

In medium saucepan melt chocolate and butterscotch chips over low heat. Remove from heat. Stir in cereal and raisins. Drop by spoonfuls onto waxed paper. Makes about 2 1/2 dozen.

Pictured on page 53.

# Saucepan Coconut Balls

*Sunflower seeds add a special nutty flavor.*

| | |
|---|---|
| Large eggs | 2 |
| Granulated sugar | 1 cup |
| Raisins | 1 cup |
| Chopped nuts | 1 cup |
| Coconut | 1 cup |
| Sunflower seeds | 1/4 cup |
| Vanilla | 1 tsp. |
| Almond flavoring | 1/8 tsp. |

Icing (confectioner's) sugar

Beat eggs in medium saucepan. Beat in sugar. Add raisins and nuts. Cook and stir over medium heat until eggs thicken. Remove from heat.

Stir in coconut, sunflower seeds, vanilla and almond flavoring. Cool.

Shape into balls. Roll in icing sugar. Freezes. Makes about 3 1/2 dozen.

Pictured on page 89.

No Bake Cookies

# Orange Balls

*These unbaked cookies have a real orange flavor.*

| | |
|---|---|
| Vanilla wafer crumbs | 4 cups |
| Butter (or hard margarine), softened | 1/2 cup |
| Icing (confectioner's) sugar | 2 1/2 cups |
| Chopped pecans or walnuts | 1/2 cup |
| Frozen concentrated orange juice, thawed | 6 oz. |
| Medium coconut or chocolate sprinkles | 2 cups |

Combine first 5 ingredients in bowl. Mix well. Shape into 1 inch balls.

Roll in coconut. Freezes well. Makes 5 dozen.

Pictured on page 89.

# Butter Balls

*Crisp and mellow with a peanut butter flavor.*

| | |
|---|---|
| Butterscotch chips | 1 cup |
| Smooth peanut butter | 1/2 cup |
| Crisp rice cereal | 3 cups |

Melt chips and peanut butter in saucepan. Stir often. Remove from heat. Mix in rice cereal. Drop by spoonfuls onto waxed paper. Makes about 3 dozen.

Pictured on page 89.

### Paré Pointer

*"Your money or your life." "Take my life. I need my money to live on."*

No Bake Cookies

# Chocolate Sandwiches

*These are crisp thin wafers put together with a creamy chocolate filling.*

| | |
|---|---|
| Butter (or hard margarine), softened | 1/2 cup |
| Granulated sugar | 1/4 cup |
| Semisweet chocolate square, melted | 1 oz. |
| All-purpose flour | 1 cup |

In mixing bowl cream together butter, sugar and chocolate.

Mix in flour. Cover and chill overnight. Roll out on lightly floured surface. Cut into squares 2 x 2 inches. Bake on greased cookie sheet in 350°F oven for about 10 to 12 minutes. When cool, put together with icing and finish as recipe states. Makes about 28 cookie sandwiches.

### ICING

| | |
|---|---|
| Butter (or hard margarine), softened | 2 tbsp. |
| Icing (confectioner's) sugar | 1/3 cup |
| Semisweet chocolate chips, melted | 1/3 cup |
| Semisweet chocolate squares, melted | 14 x 1 oz. |

With a spoon, beat first 3 ingredients together. Spread between cookies to make sandwich style.

Place a few cookies on rack over plate. Spoon semisweet chocolate over, covering tops and sides. Place on waxed paper to set. Return drained chocolate on plate back to saucepan as it collects.

Pictured on page 107.

---

### *Paré Pointer*

*The most noble dog of all is a hot dog. It feeds the hand that bites it.*

# Oatcakes

*Tender and not sweet. Traditional oatcakes used to contain lard or drippings. Today butter or hard margarine may be used.*

| | |
|---|---|
| All-purpose flour | 1 1/2 cups |
| Granulated sugar | 1/2 cup |
| Baking powder | 1 tsp. |
| Salt | 1/2 tsp. |
| Lard | 3/4 cup |
| | |
| Rolled oats | 1 1/2 cups |
| Water | 6 tbsp. |

Stir flour, sugar, baking powder and salt together in bowl. Cut in lard until crumbly.

Mix in rolled oats. Sprinkle with water. Work into a ball with your hands. Roll out fairly thin. Cut into 2 1/2 inch circles. Arrange on lightly greased cookie sheet. Bake in 350°F oven for about 15 minutes. Makes 2 1/2 dozen.

Pictured on page 125.

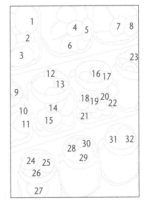

Rolled Cookies

# Lemon Cookies

*Firm and lemony.*

| | |
|---|---|
| Butter (or hard margarine), softened | 1/2 cup |
| Granulated sugar | 1/2 cup |
| Large egg | 1 |
| Sweetened condensed milk | 2/3 cup |
| Lemon juice | 2 tbsp. |
| Grated lemon rind | 1 tbsp. |
| Vanilla | 1 tsp. |
| All-purpose flour | 2 1/4 cups |
| Baking powder | 2 tsp. |
| Salt | 1/2 tsp. |

Cut butter and sugar together well. Beat in egg. Add milk, lemon juice, lemon rind and vanilla.

Stir flour, baking powder and salt together and add. Mix well. Roll out on lightly floured surface. Cut into any desired shapes from circles to Christmas trees. Bake in 350°F oven for about 8 minutes. Glaze. Makes approximately 6 dozen, 2 inch cookies.

**GLAZE**

| | |
|---|---|
| Icing (confectioner's) sugar | 3/4 cup |
| Lemon juice | 1 1/2 tsp. |
| Water | 2 tsp. |

Mix all 3 ingredients together adding more sugar or water if needed to make a barely pourable glaze. Frost cookies.

Pictured on page 107.

---

### *Paré Pointer*
*You get stucco when you sit on gummo.*

# Coffee Fingers

*These short-textured little rolls are covered with nuts.*

| | |
|---|---|
| Butter (or hard margarine), softened | 1 cup |
| Brown sugar, packed | 1/2 cup |
| Icing (confectioner's) sugar | 1/4 cup |
| Instant coffee granules, crushed | 1 tsp. |
| Egg yolk (large) | 1 |
| All-purpose flour | 2 cups |
| Egg white (large), fork beaten | 1 |
| Finely chopped nuts | 1 1/2 cups |

Measure first 5 ingredients into mixing bowl. Stir.

Add flour. Mix well. Roll 1/2 inch thick on lightly floured surface. Cut into fingers 1/2 × 2 inches.

Dip into egg white, roll in nuts and place on greased cookie sheet. Bake in 300°F oven for 20 to 25 minutes. Makes 4 dozen.

Pictured on page 107.

# Rolled Ginger Cookies

*A super dough that bakes sturdy men, lollipops and hanging ornaments. The glaze stays sticky for about thirty minutes to allow for lots of decorating trials and errors. May also be iced and decorated.*

| | |
|---|---|
| Butter (or hard margarine), softened | 1/4 cup |
| Granulated sugar | 1/2 cup |
| Molasses | 1/2 cup |
| Water | 1/3 cup |
| All-purpose flour | 3 1/4 cups |
| Baking soda | 1 tsp. |
| Ginger | 1 tsp. |
| Cinnamon | 1/2 tsp. |
| Cloves | 1/4 tsp. |
| Salt | 1/2 tsp. |
| Glaze and decorations | |

*(continued on next page)*

Rolled Cookies

In mixing bowl cream butter and sugar together. Add molasses and water.

Mix in remaining ingredients. Roll out on lightly floured board. Cut dough into shapes of gingerbread men and circles. Make hole 1/2 inch from top edge using milkshake straw.

**Lollipops:** Shape 1/3 cup dough into ball. Insert small wooden stick. Arrange on greased cookie sheet. Press with glass to 1/4 inch thick. Bake in 350°F oven for 8 to 10 minutes. Cook thicker cookies a bit longer. Makes about 2 dozen men and circles.

**Glazing and Decorating:** Brush tops of cookies with warm corn syrup. Apply decorations to your liking.

Pictured on pages 17 and 35.

# Graham Crackers

*Crisp and flavorful similar to commercial varieties.*

| | |
|---|---|
| Butter (or hard margarine), softened | 1/2 cup |
| Brown sugar, packed | 1/2 cup |
| Honey or corn syrup | 1/4 cup |
| Vanilla | 1 tsp. |
| Water | 1/2 cup |
| Graham or whole wheat flour | 2 cups |
| All-purpose flour | 1 cup |
| Baking powder | 1 tsp. |
| Baking soda | 1/2 tsp. |
| Salt | 1/2 tsp. |
| Cinnamon | 1/4 tsp. |

Measure butter, brown sugar and honey into bowl. Cream well. Add vanilla and water.

Stir remaining ingredients together and add. Mix well. Roll paper thin on lightly floured surface. Cut into 2 1/2 inch squares and place on ungreased baking sheet. Use ruler for even cutting. Prick evenly with fork. Bake in 375°F oven for about 8 to 10 minutes. Makes 7 dozen.

Pictured on page 125.

# Date Filled Oatmeal Cookies

*This makes a huge batch. They soften after being filled with date filling. Make small for tea and larger for regular use.*

| | |
|---|---|
| Butter (or hard margarine), softened | 2 cups |
| Brown sugar, packed | 2 cups |
| Milk | 1 cup |
| All-purpose flour | 4 cups |
| Rolled oats | 4 cups |
| Baking powder | 5 tsp. |
| Salt | 1 tsp. |

Cream butter and sugar together well. Slowly mix in milk.

Add remaining ingredients. Mix well. Chill for 1 hour. Roll out thinly on lightly floured board. Cut into 2 1/2 inch rounds. Place on ungreased baking sheets. Bake in 350°F oven for 8 to 10 minutes. Cool. Fill with Date Filling, below, to form sandwich cookies. Makes 15 dozen singles, 7 1/2 dozen date-filled.

**DATE FILLING**

| | |
|---|---|
| Chopped dates | 1/2 lb. |
| Granulated sugar | 1/3 cup |
| Water | 2/3 cup |

Combine dates, sugar and water in saucepan. Bring to a boil. Simmer, stirring often, until mushy. Add more water if too dry. If too runny simmer longer to evaporate moisture. Cool and spread between cookies.

Pictured on page 125.

# Jam Jams

*The best jam sandwich going.*

| | |
|---|---|
| Butter (or hard margarine), softened | 1 cup |
| Brown sugar, packed | 1/4 cup |
| Granulated sugar | 1/4 cup |
| Corn syrup | 1/2 cup |
| Large eggs | 2 |
| Vanilla | 1 tsp. |
| All-purpose flour | 3 cups |
| Baking powder | 1/2 tsp. |
| Salt | 1/2 tsp. |

Strawberry, raspberry or black currant jam or jelly

Cream butter and both sugars well. Beat in corn syrup, eggs and vanilla.

Mix in flour, baking powder and salt. Roll 1/8 inch thick on lightly floured surface. Cut in 2 3/4 inch circles. Arrange on greased cookie sheet.

Spread 1/2 tsp. jam on bottom circle leaving 3/8 inch around the outside edge bare. Cut small hole in top circle and place over jam. Press outside edge lightly with fingers. Bake in 350°F oven for 8 to 10 minutes. These may be baked separately if you prefer and sandwiched together with jam later. Makes about 20.

Pictured on page 53.

# Arrowroot Biscuits

*The addition of arrowroot flour makes this type of*
*cookie easier to digest than others.*

| | |
|---|---|
| Butter (or hard margarine), softened | 1/4 cup |
| Granulated sugar | 1/2 cup |
| Large egg | 1 |
| Vanilla | 1/2 tsp. |
| All-purpose flour | 1 cup |
| Arrowroot flour | 1/2 cup |
| Baking powder | 1/2 tsp. |
| Salt | 1/4 tsp. |

Cream butter and sugar together. Beat in egg and vanilla.

Stir remaining ingredients together and add. Mix well. Roll 1/8 inch thick on floured surface. Cut into 2 1/2 inch rounds. Place on greased baking sheet. Prick with fork. Bake in 350°F oven until golden, about 8 to 10 minutes. Allow a bit more time if rolled thicker. These do not spread. Makes 3 1/2 dozen.

Pictured on page 53.

# Peanut Wafers

*A hard thin cookie. Once you nibble on one you will find them addictive.*

| | |
|---|---|
| Large eggs | 2 |
| Ground peanuts | 2 cups |
| Granulated sugar | 1 cup |
| Butter (or hard margarine), softened | 2 tbsp. |
| Milk | 2 tbsp. |
| Salt | 1 tsp. |
| All-purpose flour | 2 cups |

Mix all ingredients together. Roll paper thin on lightly floured surface. Cut into 2 inch squares. Place on ungreased baking sheet. Bake in 375°F oven for 9 to 10 minutes. Watch carefully. They burn easily. Makes about 5 dozen.

Pictured on page 107.

Rolled Cookies

# Bourbon Cookies

*These chocolate sandwich cookies are wonderful with tea or coffee. Bourbon in the filling may be exchanged for rum or brandy flavoring.*

| | |
|---|---|
| Butter (or hard margarine), softened | 6 tbsp. |
| Granulated sugar | 1/4 cup |
| Cocoa | 1/4 cup |
| All-purpose flour | 1 1/2 cups |
| Corn syrup | 2 tbsp. |
| Large egg | 1 |

Granulated sugar for garnish

Combine butter, sugar, cocoa and flour in bowl. Mix until crumbly.

Add syrup and egg. Blend together. If necessary, add a bit more flour to make a firm dough. Knead lightly. Roll out thinly. Cut into rectangles 1 x 3 inches. Place on greased cookie sheet. Bake in 350°F oven for 10 to 15 minutes until they darken in color.

Sprinkle with sugar as soon as removed from oven. Sandwich together with filling. Makes 2 1/2 dozen.

**FILLING**

| | |
|---|---|
| Butter (or hard margarine), softened | 1/2 cup |
| Icing (confectioner's) sugar | 1 cup |
| Semisweet chocolate chips, melted and cooled | 1/3 cup |
| Bourbon (optional) | 1 tsp. |

Mix all together. Spread between cookies.

Pictured on page 143.

---

## Paré Pointer

*If you cross poison ivy with a four-leaf clover,
would you get a rash of good luck?*

# Cinnamon Rolls

*A delicious cookie that isn't too sweet.*

| | |
|---|---|
| Butter (or hard margarine), softened | 1 cup |
| Cream cheese, softened | 4 oz. |
| Granulated sugar | 3/4 cup |
| Large egg | 1 |
| Vanilla | 1 tsp. |
| All-purpose flour | 2 1/4 cups |
| Baking soda | 1/2 tsp. |
| Salt | 1/4 tsp. |
| Melted butter (or hard margarine) | 1 tbsp. |
| Cinnamon sprinkle | |
| Brown sugar sprinkle | |

Cream butter, cream cheese and sugar together well. Beat in egg and vanilla.

Stir flour, baking soda and salt together and add. Mix well. Roll dough 1/4 inch thick into rectangle about 9 x 13 inches.

Brush with melted butter. Sprinkle with cinnamon and brown sugar. Beginning at long side, roll up like a jelly roll. Chill 1/2 hour. Slice 1/4 inch thick. Arrange on greased baking sheet. Bake in 350°F oven for 10 to 12 minutes. Makes about 4 1/2 dozen.

Pictured on page 53.

# Sour Cream Nut Rolls

*Little envelopes filled with nutty almond filling.*

| | |
|---|---|
| All-purpose flour | 2 cups |
| Butter (or hard margarine), softened | 1 cup |
| Sour cream | 1/2 cup |
| Egg yolks (large) | 2 |
| FILLING | |
| Ground almonds | 2 1/2 cups |
| Granulated sugar | 1/2 cup |
| Milk | 1/4 cup |
| Almond flavoring | 1 tsp. |
| Icing (confectioner's) sugar | |

*(continued on next page)*

Rolled Cookies

Put flour and butter in large bowl. Cut in butter until crumbly.

Mix sour cream and egg yolks together with a fork to blend. Add to flour mixture. Stir and knead to form ball. Roll out 1/8 inch thick on lightly floured surface. Cut into 2 inch squares.

**Filling:** Mix almonds, sugar, milk and almond flavoring together. Place 1/2 tsp. in center of each square. Bring up 2 opposite corners. Lay 1 corner over the other, pinching to seal. Arrange on ungreased baking sheet. Bake in 400°F oven for about 10 to 12 minutes until lightly browned.

Roll in icing sugar. Makes 8 dozen.

Pictured on page 125.

# Thick White Cookies

*Big cookies, soft and thick. For a variation, sprinkle with granulated sugar before baking.*

| | |
|---|---|
| Butter (or hard margarine), softened | 1/2 cup |
| Granulated sugar | 1/2 cup |
| Brown sugar, packed | 1/2 cup |
| Large egg | 1 |
| Milk | 1/2 cup |
| Vanilla | 1 tsp. |
| All-purpose flour | 3 cups |
| Cream of tartar | 2 tsp. |
| Baking soda | 1 tsp. |
| Salt | 1/2 tsp. |

Cream butter and both sugars together. Beat in egg. Add milk and vanilla.

Stir flour, cream of tartar, baking soda and salt together and add. Mix well. Roll out 1/4 inch thick on floured surface. Cut into 2 3/4 inch rounds. Place on greased baking sheet. Bake in 375°F oven for 8 to 10 minutes. Makes 2 1/2 dozen.

Pictured on page 53.

# Boiled Egg Cookies

*This is a variation of a popular cookie in Caen. Cooked egg yolks are added to the batter.*

| | |
|---|---|
| Butter (or hard margarine), softened | 1 cup |
| Granulated sugar | 1 cup |
| Egg yolks (large) | 2 |
| All-purpose flour | 3 cups |
| Large hard-boiled eggs, mash yolks and save whites for another purpose | 4 |
| Egg whites (large), slightly beaten | 2 |
| Chopped nuts | 1/4 cup |
| Granulated sugar | 1/4 cup |

Cream butter and first amount of sugar together. Add egg yolks and flour. Mash cooked egg yolks and add to butter mixture. Mix together well. Roll on lightly floured board. Cut into 2 inch rounds. Arrange on ungreased baking sheet.

Brush cookies with egg whites. Mix nuts and remaining sugar together. Sprinkle over top. Bake in 350°F oven for 12 to 15 minutes. Makes 6 dozen.

Pictured on page 53.

# Thick Molasses Cookies

*These big old fashioned cookies are soft and thick.*

| | |
|---|---|
| Cooking oil | 1 cup |
| Granulated sugar | 1 cup |
| Large egg | 1 |
| Molasses | 1 cup |
| Milk | 1/2 cup |
| Baking soda | 2 tsp. |
| All-purpose flour | 5 1/4 cups |
| Salt | 1/2 tsp. |

*(continued on next page)*

Beat oil, sugar and egg together well. Add molasses.

Stir milk and baking soda together to dissolve and add.

Add flour and salt. Mix well. Roll out 1/4 inch thick on floured surface. Cut into 2 3/4 inch rounds. Arrange on greased baking sheet. Bake in 375°F oven for about 8 to 10 minutes. Makes 3 1/2 dozen.

Pictured on page 35.

# Cornmeal Crisps

*These have the unusual addition of cornmeal. Crispy good.*

| | |
|---|---|
| Butter (or hard margarine), softened | 1/2 cup |
| Granulated sugar | 3/4 cup |
| Large egg | 1 |
| Lemon juice | 2 tsp. |
| Grated lemon rind | 1 tsp. |
| All purpose flour | 1 1/2 cups |
| Cornmeal | 1/2 cup |
| Baking powder | 1 tsp. |
| Salt | 1/2 tsp. |
| Chopped raisins | 1/2 cup |

Cream butter and sugar together well. Beat in egg, lemon juice and rind.

Add remaining ingredients. Mix well. Roll out on lightly floured board 1/4 inch thick and cut into 2 inch circles. Dough may also be shaped into roll 2 inches in diameter and chilled. Cut into slices 1/4 inch thick. Place on greased baking sheet. Bake in 350°F oven for 9 to 12 minutes until golden. Makes 3 dozen.

Pictured on page 71.

### Paré Pointer

*No madam you can't try on that dress in the window. You will have to use a fitting room like everyone else.*

# Raisin Filled Cookies

*Serve hot from the oven for an extra special delight. Dough and filling can be kept refrigerated to bake as needed if desired.*

FILLING

| | |
|---|---|
| Raisins, coarsely chopped | 1 1/2 cups |
| Granulated sugar | 3/4 cup |
| Cornstarch | 1 tbsp. |
| Water | 3/4 cup |
| Lemon juice | 1 1/2 tsp. |

COOKIE DOUGH

| | |
|---|---|
| Butter (or hard margarine), softened | 1 cup |
| Granulated sugar | 1 1/2 cups |
| Large eggs | 2 |
| Vanilla | 1 tsp. |
| All-purpose flour | 3 1/2 cups |
| Baking soda | 1 tsp. |
| Salt | 1/2 tsp. |

**Granulated sugar for garnish**

**Filling:** Mix all ingredients together in saucepan. Bring to a boil, stirring over medium heat. Cool.

**Cookie Dough:** Cream butter and sugar together. Beat in eggs 1 at a time. Add vanilla.

Stir flour, baking soda and salt together and add. Mix well. Roll out thinly on floured surface. Cut into 2 1/2 inch circles. Arrange circles on greased baking sheet. Drop 1 tsp. raisin filling in center. Cover with second circle. Press edges with floured fork.

Cut a cross in top center about 1/2 to 3/4 inch each way.

Sprinkle with sugar. Bake in 350°F oven until lightly browned, about 10 minutes. Makes 4 dozen.

Pictured on page 107.

Rolled Cookies

# High Hats

*Marshmallow halves top chocolate cookie bases then melted chocolate is drizzled over all.*

| | |
|---|---|
| Butter (or hard margarine), softened | 1/2 cup |
| Granulated sugar | 1/2 cup |
| Large egg | 1 |
| Sour cream | 1/2 cup |
| Vanilla | 1/2 tsp. |
| All-purpose flour | 1 3/4 cups |
| Cocoa | 1/3 cup |
| Baking powder | 1/2 tsp. |
| Baking soda | 1/4 tsp. |
| Salt | 1/4 tsp. |
| Large marshmallows, halved | 32 |
| Semisweet chocolate chips | 1 cup |
| Grated parowax (paraffin) | 2 tbsp. |
| Butter (or hard margarine) | 1 tbsp. |

Cream butter and sugar together in bowl. Beat in egg. Add sour cream and vanilla. Mix.

Stir flour, cocoa, baking powder, baking soda and salt together. Add to sour cream mixture. Mix well. On lightly floured surface roll out dough to 1/8 inch thickness. Cut into 2 inch rounds. Place on lightly greased baking sheet. Bake in 350°F oven for 10 to 12 minutes.

Cut marshmallows in half. Scissors do this well. Place marshmallow half in center of hot cookie immediately upon removal from oven. Let stand to cool.

**Coating:** Melt chocolate chips, wax and butter in small saucepan over low heat. Spoon over top of marshmallow while holding cookie or place cookie in sieve over a plate and pour chocolate over top. Place on waxed paper to set.

**Variation:** A dab of red jam or half a nut may be hidden underneath each marshmallow.

Pictured on page 125.

# Lebkuchen

*Layb-COO-cun is a popular well known German Christmas cookie. Leave plain, glaze, or glaze and decorate. Pretty and spicy. No fat in these.*

| | |
|---|---|
| Honey | 2/3 cup |
| Molasses | 1/3 cup |
| | |
| Large egg | 1 |
| Brown sugar, packed | 3/4 cup |
| Lemon juice | 2 tbsp. |
| Chopped candied citron | 1/2 cup |
| Finely chopped almonds | 1/3 cup |
| | |
| All-purpose flour | 3 1/2 cups |
| Cinnamon | 1 tsp. |
| Salt | 1/2 tsp. |
| Baking soda | 1/2 tsp. |
| Nutmeg | 1/2 tsp. |
| Cloves | 1/2 tsp. |

**Flaked almonds, cherries, corn syrup for garnish**

Bring honey and molasses to a boil in small saucepan. Remove from heat.

Beat egg in mixing bowl until frothy. Beat in sugar. Add lemon juice, citron, almonds and hot honey-molasses mixture.

Stir next 6 ingredients together and add. Mix well. Roll out 1/4 inch thick on floured surface. Cut in 2 1/2 inch circles. Place on greased cookie sheet.

Decorate with flaked almonds and bits of cherries. A dab of corn syrup helps them stick. Bake in 375°F oven for about 8 to 10 minutes. Cool. Brush with warm corn syrup to glaze. Makes about 3 1/2 dozen.

Pictured on page 17.

---

## Paré Pointer

*They tried to kiss in a dense fog. They mist.*

# Teething Biscuits

*Make your own baby cookies. These are hard and tasty.*

| | |
|---|---|
| Large eggs | 2 |
| Granulated sugar | 1 cup |
| Vanilla | 1 tsp. |
| All-purpose flour | 2 cups |

Beat eggs in medium size bowl until frothy. Add sugar, vanilla and 2 cups flour. Mix together. Work in additional flour as needed to make a stiff dough. Roll 1/4 inch thick. Cut into rings and sticks. Place on greased cookie sheet. Let stand uncovered overnight to dry. Next morning bake in 325°F oven for about 30 minutes until dry and hard. Cool thoroughly before storing. Makes about 2 dozen.

Pictured on page 89.

# Wholemeal Wafers

*A crisp wafer to munch. Not sweet.*

| | |
|---|---|
| Whole wheat flour | 2 cups |
| Rolled oats, ground | 1/2 cup |
| Brown sugar, packed | 1/4 cup |
| Baking powder | 1 tsp. |
| Salt | 1 tsp. |
| Butter (or hard margarine), softened | 1/2 cup |
| Large eggs | 2 |
| Water | 2 tbsp. |

Crumble first 6 ingredients together in bowl until mealy texture.

Put eggs and water into small container. With a fork beat until well mixed. Add to bowl. Mix as for pie crust until it forms a ball. Roll out paper thin on lightly floured surface. Cut into 2 1/2 inch circles. Place on greased cookie sheet. Pierce with fork. Bake in 350°F oven for about 10 minutes until browned. Makes 6 dozen.

Pictured on page 125.

# Candy Cane Cookies

*A fun cookie for all the family to make together.*

| | |
|---|---|
| Butter (or hard margarine), softened | 1 cup |
| Icing (confectioner's) sugar | 1 cup |
| Large egg | 1 |
| Almond flavoring | 1 tsp. |
| Vanilla flavoring | 1 tsp. |
| Peppermint flavoring | 1/4 tsp. |
| All-purpose flour | 2 1/2 cups |
| Baking powder | 1 tsp. |
| Salt | 1 tsp. |
| Red food coloring | 1/2 tsp. |

Mix first 6 ingredients together well.

Add flour, baking powder and salt. Mix well.

Divide dough into 2 equal portions. Add food coloring to 1 portion. Blend well. Roll 1 tsp. of each color dough into ropes about 5 1/2 inches long. Lay them side by side. Pinch ends together. Twist to form a spiral. Lay on ungreased baking sheet. Shape to form a cane. Wreaths are easy to make too. Bake in 350°F oven for about 10 minutes until pale gold. Cool on sheet 2 to 3 minutes then remove. Makes about 4 1/2 dozen.

Pictured on page 17.

# Sacher Torte Bites

*These cookies have the flavor combination of the famous Viennese torte.*

| | |
|---|---|
| Butter (or hard margarine), softened | 1 cup |
| Instant chocolate pudding, 4 serving size | 1 |
| Large egg | 1 |
| All-purpose flour | 2 cups |
| Granulated sugar | 1/4 cup |
| Apricot jam | 1/2 cup |
| Semisweet chocolate chips | 1/2 cup |
| Butter (or hard margarine) | 3 tbsp. |

Cream butter and pudding powder together. Beat in egg. Mix in flour. Shape into small balls.

Roll balls in sugar. Place on greased baking sheet. Make a dent in each with your thumb. Bake in 325°F oven for 5 minutes. Remove cookies and press dent again. Continue baking for about 10 to 15 minutes.

Fill dents with jam. Melt chocolate and butter in small saucepan over low heat. Stir to hasten melting. Glaze tops of cooled cookies. Makes 4 dozen.

**BLACK FOREST COOKIES:** Fill with 1/2 maraschino cherry or with cherry jam instead of apricot.

Pictured on page 143.

# Ranger Cookies

*Chewy and nutritious. Good for snacks, lunch boxes and pockets.*

| | |
|---|---|
| Butter (or hard margarine), softened | 1 cup |
| Granulated sugar | 1 cup |
| Brown sugar | 1 cup |
| Large eggs | 2 |
| Vanilla | 2 tsp. |
| | |
| All-purpose flour | 2 cups |
| Baking soda | 1 tsp. |
| Baking powder | 1/2 tsp. |
| Salt | 1 1/2 tsp. |
| | |
| Crisp rice cereal | 2 cups |
| Rolled oats | 2 cups |
| Coconut | 1 cup |
| Raisins | 1 cup |

Cream butter and both sugars together. Beat in eggs 1 at a time. Add vanilla.

Stir flour, baking soda, baking powder and salt together and add. Mix.

Add cereal, oats, coconut and raisins. Mix well. Dough will be thick. Roll into 1 inch balls or push off pieces of dough from spoon. Arrange on greased baking sheet. Bake in 375°F oven for 6 to 8 minutes until golden. Makes 8 dozen.

Pictured on page 125.

---

### Paré Pointer
*You should pay your taxes with a smile. Too bad they insist on cash.*

# Ginger Snaps

*These snaps have crackle tops and a spicy bite to them. An old timer.*

| | |
|---|---|
| Butter (or hard margarine), softened | 3/4 cup |
| Granulated sugar | 1 cup |
| Large egg | 1 |
| Molasses | 1/2 cup |
| All-purpose flour | 2 1/2 cups |
| Baking soda | 2 tsp. |
| Ginger | 2 tsp. |
| Cinnamon | 1 tsp. |
| Salt | 1/2 tsp. |
| Granulated sugar | |

Cream butter and first amount of sugar well. Beat in egg. Mix in molasses.

Stir flour, baking soda, ginger, cinnamon and salt together and add. Mix well. Shape into 1 inch balls.

Roll in sugar and place on greased baking sheet. Bake in 350°F oven for 10 to 12 minutes. Makes 6 dozen.

Pictured on page 71.

# Coconut Crisps

*Easy to prepare with few ingredients. The result is a tasty crisp cookie. When dipped in chocolate they become tiny chocolate bars.*

| | |
|---|---|
| Butter (or hard margarine), softened | 1 cup |
| Granulated sugar | 1/2 cup |
| Vanilla | 1 tsp. |
| All-purpose flour | 2 cups |
| Coconut | 1 cup |

Cream butter, sugar and vanilla well.

Add flour and coconut. Mix together to form a ball. Shape into small balls. Place on greased cookie sheet. Press with fork. Bake in 350°F oven for 12 to 15 minutes. Makes 2 1/2 to 3 dozen.

Pictured on page 125.

# Chocolate Chip Shortbread

*A scrumptious variation of a popular cookie.*

| | |
|---|---|
| Butter (not margarine), softened | 1 cup |
| Brown sugar, packed | 1/2 cup |
| Vanilla | 1 tsp. |
| All-purpose flour | 2 cups |
| Semisweet chocolate chips | 1 cup |

Measure butter, sugar, vanilla and flour into bowl. Work together until it forms a ball.

Add chocolate chips and work into dough. Roll into 1 inch balls. Place on ungreased cookie sheet. Press with fork. Bake in 325°F oven for 10 to 15 minutes. Makes 5 dozen.

Pictured on page 89.

# Ladyfingers

*Delicate and golden in color. A tea cookie.*

| | |
|---|---|
| Egg whites (large), room temperature | 3 |
| Granulated sugar | 1/4 cup |
| Egg yolks (large) | 3 |
| Vanilla | 1 tsp. |
| Granulated sugar | 1/4 cup |
| All-purpose flour | 2/3 cup |

In mixing bowl beat egg whites until soft peaks form. Add first amount of sugar gradually, beating until stiff.

In another bowl beat egg yolks, vanilla and second amount of sugar until a light cream color. Fold into egg whites.

Sprinkle flour over top. Fold in. Pipe into strips about 1/2 x 2 1/2 inches onto greased baking sheet. Bake in 350°F oven for about 10 minutes. Watch carefully so they don't burn. Makes about 3 1/2 dozen.

Pictured on page 143.

# Biscuit Cookies

*A yummy cookie destined to be in many a lunchbox. Quick to make.*

| | |
|---|---|
| Refrigerated crescent rolls | 1 pkg. |
| Smooth peanut butter | 8 tsp. |
| Granulated sugar | 4 tsp. |
| Semisweet chocolate chips | 8 tsp. |

Granulated sugar

Spread each triangle of dough with 1 tsp. peanut butter. Sprinkle each with 1/2 tsp. sugar followed by 1 tsp. chocolate chips. Roll from shortest side enclosing all chips as you roll.

Roll in sugar and place on ungreased cookie sheet. Bake in 375°F oven for 10 to 12 minutes. Makes 8.

Pictured on page 125.

# Mint Surprise

*Bite into this tasty cookie and find a creamy mint hidden inside.*

| | |
|---|---|
| Butter (or hard margarine), softened | 1/2 cup |
| Granulated sugar | 1/2 cup |
| Brown sugar, packed | 1/4 cup |
| Large egg | 1 |
| Vanilla | 1/2 tsp. |
| All-purpose flour | 1 1/2 cups |
| Graham cracker crumbs | 1/4 cup |
| Baking soda | 1/2 tsp. |
| Salt | 1/2 tsp. |

Solid mint-flavored chocolate wafers
or colored cream mints

Cream butter and both sugars together. Beat in egg and vanilla.

Add flour, crumbs, baking soda and salt. Mix well.

Wrap each mint in about 1 1/2 tsp. dough. Arrange on ungreased baking sheet. Bake in 375°F oven for 8 to 10 minutes until lightly browned. Makes about 5 dozen.

Pictured on page 107.

# Spritz Cookies

*Put through a cookie press. These are either decorated before baking,*
*left plain or dipped in melted chocolate. Nice and crisp.*

| | |
|---|---|
| Butter (or hard margarine), softened | 1 cup |
| Granulated sugar | 1 cup |
| Large eggs | 2 |
| Vanilla | 1 1/2 tsp. |
| | |
| All-purpose flour | 3 cups |
| Baking powder | 1/2 tsp. |
| Salt | 1/4 tsp. |

Cream butter and sugar together well. Beat in eggs, 1 at a time. Add vanilla.

Stir in flour, baking powder and salt. Force dough through cookie press onto ungreased cookie sheet. Decorate with small colored sugar beads if desired. Bake in 400°F oven for about 10 to 12 minutes until edges begin to brown. Makes 6 to 7 dozen.

**CHOCOLATE SPRITZ:** Exchange 6 tbsp. of flour for an equal amount of cocoa.

**ORANGE SPRITZ:** Add 2 tsp. grated orange rind and 1/2 tsp. orange flavoring.

**ALMOND SPRITZ:** Add 1 tsp. almond flavoring.

**CHOCOLATE ORANGE SPRITZ:** Exchange 6 tbsp. of flour for an equal amount of cocoa. Add 2 tsp. orange extract. Good.

**CHOCOLATE FILLING**

| | |
|---|---|
| Semisweet chocolate chips, melted | 1/3 cup |
| Butter (or hard margarine), softened | 1 tbsp. |
| Icing (confectioner's) sugar | 2 tbsp. |

Mix all together. Use to sandwich cookies. Makes a scant 1/2 cup.

**PEANUT BUTTER FILLING**

| | |
|---|---|
| Smooth peanut butter | 1/4 cup |
| Butter (or hard margarine), softened | 1 tbsp. |
| Icing (confectioner's) sugar | 2 tbsp. |

Mix together well. Spread between 2 thin cookies. Makes a scant 1/3 cup.

Pictured on page 107.

# Peppernuts

*Put out a bowlful of these spicy little cookies. Makes a nice
snack with coffee. These contain no fat.*

| | |
|---|---|
| Large eggs | 3 |
| Granulated sugar | 1 cup |
| Brown sugar, packed | 1 cup |
| All-purpose flour | 2 3/4 cups |
| Baking powder | 1 tsp. |
| Cinnamon | 1 tsp. |
| Allspice | 1/2 tsp. |
| Nutmeg | 1/2 tsp. |
| Cloves | 1/4 tsp. |
| Pepper, white or black | 1/4 tsp. |
| Grated lemon rind | 1 1/2 tsp. |
| Finely chopped almonds | 1/2 cup |

In mixing bowl beat eggs until frothy. Add both sugars. Beat until very
light and fluffy, at least 5 or 6 minutes.

Add all remaining ingredients. Mix together well. Roll into ropes 1/2 inch
in diameter. Slice into pieces 1/2 inch long. Arrange on greased sheet. Bake
in 325°F oven for 15 minutes until browned. Makes 8 or 9 dozen.

Pictured on page 143.

## Paré Pointer

*Someone cut a large hole in the fence around the nudist camp. The
police are looking into it.*

# Pretzels

*These are easy to make. A different shape for cookies. Tasty.*
*May be dipped in melted chocolate.*

| | |
|---|---|
| Butter (or hard margarine), softened | 1/2 cup |
| Granulated sugar | 1/2 cup |
| Large egg | 1 |
| Corn syrup | 2 tbsp. |
| All-purpose flour | 2 cups |
| Baking powder | 1 tsp. |
| Salt | 1/8 tsp. |

Cream butter and sugar together. Beat in egg. Add corn syrup.

Stir flour, baking powder and salt together and add. Mix well. Shape into 7 inch pencil size ropes. Form into a horseshoe. Bring ends down to center of rope overlapping and pressing ends forming pretzel shape. Arrange on greased cookie sheet. These hold their shape much better if chilled for 1/2 hour or so at this point. Bake in 375°F oven for 10 to 12 minutes.

Pictured on page 107.

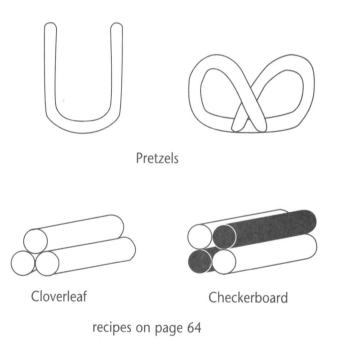

Pretzels

Cloverleaf                    Checkerboard

recipes on page 64

# War-Time Cookies

*During World War II when sugar was scarce, people were in luck if a pudding powder was available. This is still a favorite today. Not too sweet.*

| | |
|---|---|
| Butterscotch or caramel pudding powder, 4 serving size, not instant | 1 |
| Butter (or hard margarine), softened | 3/4 cup |
| Granulated sugar | 1 tbsp. |
| All-purpose flour | 1 cup |
| Rolled oats | 1 1/2 cups |
| Baking powder | 1/4 tsp. |
| Baking soda | 1/4 tsp. |
| Salt | 1/8 tsp. |
| Vanilla | 1 tsp. |
| Large egg | 1 |

In mixing bowl, add and mix ingredients in order given. Roll into balls, 1 to 1 1/4 inches in diameter. Place on greased baking sheet. Press with fork. Bake in 375°F oven for 10 to 15 minutes. Makes about 3 dozen.

Pictured on page 71.

# Crackerjack Cookies

*Crunchy and good to please any age. A real crackerjack of a cookie.*

| | |
|---|---|
| Butter (or hard margarine), softened | 1 cup |
| Brown sugar, packed | 1 cup |
| Granulated sugar | 1 cup |
| Large eggs | 2 |
| Vanilla | 2 tsp. |
| Rolled oats | 2 cups |
| Crisp rice cereal | 2 cups |
| All-purpose flour | 1 1/2 cups |
| Coconut | 1 cup |
| Baking powder | 1 tsp. |
| Baking soda | 1 tsp. |

Mix first 5 ingredients together well.

Add remaining ingredients. Mix together. Shape into balls. Do not flatten. Arrange on ungreased baking sheet. Bake in 375°F oven for 8 to 10 minutes. Makes about 6 dozen.

Pictured on pages 71 and 89.

# Fortune Cookies

*Making these from scratch enables you to write your own fortune.*
*These are great conversation cookies.*

| | |
|---|---|
| All-purpose flour | 3/4 cup |
| Granulated sugar | 1 cup |
| Salt | 1/4 tsp. |
| Butter (or hard margarine), melted | 1/2 cup |
| Egg whites (4 large) | 1/2 cup |
| Vanilla | 1 tsp. |
| Fortunes typed on paper strips | |

Stir flour, sugar, and salt together in bowl.

Add remaining ingredients. Beat until smooth. Drop level teaspoonfuls onto greased baking sheet leaving a lot of room for expansion. Bake in 300°F oven for 12 to 15 minutes. Fold immediately using tea towel to protect hands from heat. Fold top edges together.

Insert fortune on bottom. Have bottom well ballooned apart. Press cookie over thin object such as side of thin saucepan. Place in muffin tin to ensure they will hold their shape as they cool. Makes 3 1/2 dozen.

Pictured on page 107.

# Brandy Snaps

*These fragile cookies are baked flat, rolled hot and*
*filled cold. An extra special treat.*

| | |
|---|---|
| Butter (or hard margarine) | 1/4 cup |
| Granulated sugar | 1/4 cup |
| Corn syrup | 2 tbsp. |
| | |
| All-purpose flour | 1/2 cup |
| Ginger | 1/2 tsp. |
| Brandy flavoring | 1 tsp. |
| Water | 4 tsp. |
| | |
| FILLING | |
| Whipping cream | 1 cup |
| Granulated sugar | 1 tbsp. |
| Brandy flavoring | 1/2 tsp. |

Put butter, first amount of sugar and syrup in saucepan. Heat and stir until sugar is dissolved.

Remove from heat. Add flour, ginger, brandy flavoring and water. Mix well. Drop by teaspoonfuls onto greased baking sheet allowing room for expansion. Make 4 at once to allow for proper handling. Bake in 350°F oven for about 6 to 7 minutes or until edges are golden. Cool 1 minute. Working quickly, loosen 1 cookie. With rough (top) side out, roll around wooden spoon handle to shape. Ease off onto counter. Repeat. If cookies harden too much to remove, put back in oven to heat. These can be kept for a few days or frozen.

**Filling:** To serve, whip cream, second amount of sugar and brandy flavoring until stiff. Spoon or pipe into rolls. Serve at once. Makes about 16.

**Note:** To use brandy in cookies omit brandy flavoring and water. Add 2 tbsp. brandy. For filling, omit brandy flavoring and add 1 tbsp. brandy.

Pictured on page 143.

# Slow Pokes

*Baked long at a low temperature, these cookies shatter and melt in your mouth. A yummy caramel flavor.*

| | |
|---|---|
| Butter (or hard margarine), softened | 1 cup |
| Granulated sugar | 1 cup |
| Egg yolk (large) | 1 |
| Vanilla | 2 tsp. |
| | |
| All-purpose flour | 2 cups |
| Salt | 1/4 tsp. |
| Baking powder | 1 tsp. |
| Hot water | 2 tsp. |
| Baking soda | 1 tsp. |
| | |
| Egg white (large) | 1 |
| Finely chopped pecans or walnuts | 1/2 cup |

Cream butter and sugar together. Add egg yolk and vanilla.

Mix in flour, salt and baking powder. Stir hot water and baking soda together and add. Mix well. Press thinly onto 2 ungreased baking sheets.

Beat egg white until frothy. Brush over top to glaze. Sprinkle with nuts. Bake in 250°F oven for 1 hour. Cut into bars 1 1/2 × 2 1/2 inches as soon as they come from the oven. They will crumble if cut when cooled. Makes about 5 dozen.

Pictured on page 17.

### Paré Pointer

*He doesn't mind being at the bottom of the class. They teach the same thing at both ends.*

# Delights

*Tender little cookies baked in tiny muffin or tart tins. A combination of jam and nuts fills the centers.*

| | |
|---|---|
| Butter (or hard margarine), softened | 1/2 cup |
| Granulated sugar | 3/4 cup |
| Large eggs | 2 |
| All-purpose flour | 2 cups |
| Baking powder | 2 tsp. |
| Raspberry jam | 1 cup |
| Chopped nuts | 1/2 cup |

Cream butter and sugar together. Beat in eggs, 1 at a time. Stir in flour and baking powder. Form into round balls, about 36. Place in small greased muffin tins. Press around the edges of each cup.

Mix jam and nuts together. Fill centers with this mixture. Bake in 350°F oven for 10 to 15 minutes until edges begin to brown. Makes 3 dozen.

Pictured on page 143.

# Tea Time Rolls

*Crisp and dainty, these are special rolled tea cookies. Good served with ice cream, or may be filled with whipped cream.*

| | |
|---|---|
| Egg whites (large), room temperature | 2 |
| Granulated sugar | 1/2 cup |
| All-purpose flour | 1/2 cup |
| Butter (or hard margarine), melted and cooled | 1/4 cup |
| Grated rind of orange | 1 |
| Milk | 1/2 cup |

Beat egg whites until soft peaks form. Gradually beat in sugar until stiff.

Fold in remaining ingredients 1 at a time, in order given. Drop by teaspoonfuls onto greased baking sheet. Make only 4 at a time. Bake in 375°F oven for 6 to 7 minutes until browned on edges. Roll while hot around spoon handle or cone shaped object. If cookies harden too quickly, put back in oven to heat. Makes 2 1/2 dozen.

Pictured on page 143.

# Easy Fig Newtons

*Make your own with as much or as little filling as you like. Very tasty.*

| FILLING | |
|---|---|
| Dried figs, ground | 1 lb. |
| Water | 1/2 cup |
| Granulated sugar | 1/4 cup |
| Lemon juice | 2 tbsp. |

| DOUGH | |
|---|---|
| Butter (or hard margarine), softened | 1/2 cup |
| Brown sugar, packed | 1 cup |
| Large eggs | 2 |
| Vanilla | 1 tsp. |
| All-purpose flour | 2 cups |
| Baking powder | 1/2 tsp. |
| Baking soda | 1/2 tsp. |
| Salt | 1/2 tsp. |

**Filling:** Combine all ingredients in saucepan. Bring to a boil. Simmer for about 5 minutes or so, stirring often. Cool well. Figs may be chopped instead of ground before boiling and then run through blender or food processor before cooling. Add more water if needed.

**Dough:** Cream butter and sugar together well. Beat in eggs 1 at a time. Add vanilla.

Stir remaining ingredients together and add. Mix well. Divide dough into 2 portions. Chill for about 1 hour. Roll 1 portion thinly on lightly floured surface into rectangle 9 x 15 inches. Using ruler to measure, cut rectangle into 3 long strips each of equal width. Spoon 1/6 of filling down center of each. Fold sides of dough over filling, overlapping enough to seal. Place overlapped side down on greased baking sheet. Cut into 1 1/2 inch lengths but do not separate. Bake in 350°F oven for 15 to 20 minutes until lightly browned. Cut through to bottom again between each cookie, then remove from baking sheet. Makes 5 dozen.

Pictured on page 89.

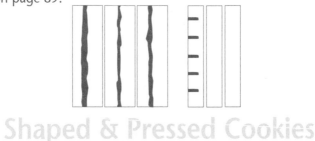

# Molasses Rolls

*Crisp dark-colored cookies that are rolled after baking. These are tasty left plain but may also be filled with whipped cream.*

| | |
|---|---|
| Butter (or hard margarine) | 1/4 cup |
| Granulated sugar | 1/2 cup |
| Table molasses | 3/4 cup |
| All-purpose flour | 1 cup |
| Salt | 3/4 tsp. |

Melt butter in saucepan. Add sugar and molasses. Stir and bring to a boil. Cool for about 5 minutes.

Stir in flour and salt. Drop by teaspoonfuls onto greased baking sheet. Bake in 350°F oven for 8 to 9 minutes. Watch carefully. These darken very fast. As soon as cookie can be removed from sheet, about 1 minute, roll around finger or spoon handle. If they harden before you finish rolling them, put back in oven to heat. Bake only 4 at a time for easy handling. Makes about 3 1/2 dozen.

Pictured on page 53.

# Butter Thins

*Buttery rich, these resemble little saddles.*

| | |
|---|---|
| Butter, softened | 1/4 cup |
| Granulated sugar | 1/2 cup |
| Vanilla | 1/2 tsp. |
| Egg white (large) | 1 |
| All-purpose flour | 1/3 cup |

Cream butter and sugar together. Stir in vanilla, egg white and flour. Drop by 1 1/2 teaspoonfuls onto greased baking sheet. Make only 4 at a time. Bake in 350°F oven for 5 to 6 minutes. Let stand on baking sheet for about 1 minute. Remove and press gently over rolling pin to shape. Makes about 20.

Pictured on page 125.

# Chocolate Walnut Logs

*These perky little chocolate logs have one end coated in nuts.*

| Butter (or hard margarine), softened | 1/2 cup |
| Granulated sugar | 1/4 cup |
| Cocoa | 2 tbsp. |
| Vanilla | 1 tsp. |
| Salt | 1/8 tsp. |
| Egg yolk (large) | 1 |
| All-purpose flour | 1 cup |

COATING
| Egg white (large), lightly beaten | 1 |
| Finely chopped walnuts | 1/4 cup |
| Granulated sugar | 2 tbsp. |

Measure first 6 ingredients into mixing bowl. Beat until fluffy.

Stir in flour. Roll into ropes. Cut into 2 inch lengths.

**Coating:** Dip 1 end of each log in egg white, then in mixture of nuts and sugar. Arrange on greased baking sheet about 1 inch apart. Bake in 350°F oven for about 15 minutes. Makes 4 dozen.

Pictured on page 17.

# Pecan Balls

*These tender little balls melt in your mouth. They are sometimes known ⌐*
*Mexican Wedding Cakes or Russian Tea Cakes.*

| | |
|---|---|
| Butter (or hard margarine), softened | 1 cup |
| Icing (confectioner's) sugar | 1/2 cup |
| All-purpose flour | 2 1/4 cups |
| Ground pecans | 1 cup |
| Vanilla | 2 tsp. |
| Icing (confectioner's) sugar | 1/2 cup |

Combine first 5 ingredients in bowl. Mix first with spoon then by hand to work it until it holds together. Shape into 1 inch balls. Arrange on ungreased baking sheet. Bake in 325°F oven for 20 to 25 minutes.

As soon as balls have cooled enough to handle, roll them in icing sugar. Makes about 6 dozen.

**ALMOND BALLS:** Omit pecans. Add 1 cup ground almonds.

**ALMOND CRESCENTS:** Omit pecans. Add 2 cups ground almonds. Roll into ropes as thick as your finger. Cut into 2 inch lengths. Pinch ends to taper. Shape into crescents.

**BURIED CHERRY:** Completely cover well drained maraschino cherries with dough. Bake same as above.

Pictured on page 17.

### Paré Pointer
*A suitable greeting for a bird with webbed feet would be*
*"What's up, duck?"*

# 'e Chocolate Chippers

*These are a chocoholic's delight.*

|  |  |
|---|---|
|  | 4 |
|  | 1 3/4 cups |
|  | 1 cup |
| ₋etened chocolate squares, melted | 4 x 1 oz. |
| vanilla | 1 tsp. |
| All-purpose flour | 3 1/2 cups |
| Baking powder | 2 tsp. |
| Salt | 1/4 tsp. |
| Semisweet chocolate chips | 1 cup |
| Icing (confectioner's) sugar, optional | 1 cup |

Beat eggs until frothy. Add sugar and beat. Mix in cooking oil, chocolate and vanilla.

Add flour, baking powder, salt and chips. Stir to mix.

Roll into 1 inch balls and then into icing sugar, if desired. Place on greased sheet. Bake in 350°F oven for 8 to 10 minutes. Do not overbake. Makes 6 dozen.

Pictured on page 53.

# Potato Chip Cookies

*Try your chips in a cookie instead of using with a dip.*

| Butter (or hard margarine), softened | 1/2 cup |
|---|---|
| Granulated sugar | 1/2 cup |
| Brown sugar, packed | 1/2 cup |
| Large egg | 1 |
| Vanilla | 1/2 tsp. |
| All-purpose flour | 1 cup |
| Baking soda | 1/2 tsp. |
| Crushed potato chips | 1 cup |
| Chopped pecans | 1/2 cup |

Cream butter and both sugars together well. Beat in egg and vanilla.

Add remaining ingredients. Mix well. Roll into 1 inch balls. Place on ungreased baking sheet. Leave as is or flatten with glass dipped in granulated sugar. Bake in 350°F oven for 10 to 12 minutes. Makes 3 dozen.

Pictured on page 71.

# Angel Cookies

*A light crisp cookie perfect for tea.*

| | |
|---|---|
| Butter (or hard margarine), softened | 1 cup |
| Granulated sugar | 1/2 cup |
| Brown sugar, packed | 1/2 cup |
| Large egg | 1 |
| Vanilla | 1 tsp. |
| All-purpose flour | 2 cups |
| Cream of tartar | 1 tsp. |
| Baking soda | 1 tsp. |
| Salt | 1/4 tsp. |

Cream butter and both sugars together well. Beat in egg and vanilla.

Stir remaining ingredients together and add. Mix. Shape into 1 inch balls. Arrange on ungreased cookie sheet. Press with fork. Bake in 350°F oven for 8 to 10 minutes until golden. Makes 5 dozen.

**Variation:** Add cherries, nuts, chocolate chips or raisins.

Pictured on page 143.

# Chocolate Snaps

*These resemble ginger snaps in appearance. Crisp enough for dunking.*

| | |
|---|---|
| Large eggs | 2 |
| Butter (or hard margarine), softened | 1/2 cup |
| Chocolate cake mix, 2 layer size, (Devil's food is best) | 1 |
| Icing (confectioner's) sugar or granulated sugar (optional) | |

Beat eggs with spoon. Add butter and cake mix. Stir together well. Shape into 1 inch balls.

Roll in sugar if desired. Place on greased cookie sheet. Bake in 375°F oven for 8 to 10 minutes. Let stand 1 minute. Remove to cool on racks. Makes about 4 dozen.

Pictured on page 53.

# Jam Diagonals

*Pretty as a picture. Saves time by baking in strips and cutting into cookies before cooling.*

| | |
|---|---|
| Butter (or hard margarine), softened | 1 cup |
| Granulated sugar | 1/2 cup |
| Large egg | 1 |
| Vanilla | 1 tsp. |
| Lemon flavoring | 1/4 tsp. |
| All-purpose flour | 2 1/2 cups |
| Baking powder | 1/2 tsp. |
| Salt | 1/4 tsp. |
| Raspberry jam, sieved | 1/3 cup |

Cream butter and sugar in bowl. Beat in egg, vanilla and lemon flavoring.

Stir flour, baking powder and salt together. Add and mix. Divide dough into 8 portions. Make each into a rope about 10 inches long and 3/4 inch wide. Place on ungreased baking sheet. With side of your hand, press to indent along center lengthwise of each strip.

Spread seedless raspberry jam in indentations. Bake in 350°F oven for 15 to 17 minutes. Cut while warm into 1 inch diagonal slices. Makes about 5 dozen.

Pictured on page 107.

# Anise Drops

*These moist drops have a mild licorice flavor to them. Pleasant and different.*

| | |
|---|---|
| Butter (or hard margarine), softened | 1/4 cup |
| Granulated sugar | 3/4 cup |
| Large eggs | 2 |
| Aniseed | 2 tbsp. |
| Grated lemon rind | 1 tsp. |
| All-purpose flour | 2 cups |
| Baking powder | 1 tbsp. |
| Salt | 1/2 tsp. |

*(continued on next page)*

Cream butter and sugar together. Beat in eggs 1 at a time. Stir in aniseed and lemon rind.

Stir flour, baking powder and salt together and add. Mix well. Shape into 1 inch balls. Place on greased cookie sheet. Press with floured fork. Bake in 375°F oven for 8 to 10 minutes. Glaze. Makes 3 dozen.

**GLAZE:** Mix lemon juice with 1 cup icing (confectioner's) sugar to make barely pourable glaze. Spoon over cookies allowing some to run down sides.

Pictured on page 53.

# Chocolate Crinkles

*Rolled in powdered sugar and baked in small balls, these cookies turn out crackly and white.*

| | |
|---|---|
| Butter (or hard margarine), softened | 1/4 cup |
| Granulated sugar | 2 cups |
| Large eggs | 3 |
| Vanilla | 2 tsp. |
| Unsweetened chocolate squares, melted | 4 x 1 oz. |
| All-purpose flour | 2 1/2 cups |
| Baking powder | 2 tsp. |
| Salt | 1/2 tsp. |
| Icing (confectioner's) sugar | 1 cup |

Cream butter and sugar together. Beat in eggs, 1 at a time. Mix in vanilla and chocolate.

Stir flour, baking powder and salt together. Add and mix well. Shape into 1 inch balls.

Roll balls in icing sugar. Coat well. Arrange on greased baking sheet. Bake in 350°F oven for 8 to 12 minutes. Cookies will be soft. Makes 6 dozen.

Pictured on page 35.

# Pop's Cookies

*Light and crunchy. Excellent choice.*

| | |
|---|---|
| Butter (or hard margarine), softened | 1 cup |
| Granulated sugar | 1 cup |
| Brown sugar, packed | 1/2 cup |
| Large egg | 1 |
| Vanilla | 1 tsp. |
| Shredded wheat biscuits, crushed | 2 |
| Rolled oats | 1 1/2 cups |
| All-purpose flour | 1 1/2 cups |
| Baking powder | 1 tsp. |
| Baking soda | 1 tsp. |

In mixing bowl, cream butter and both sugars together well. Beat in egg and vanilla.

Add crushed shredded wheat — measures 2/3 cup — and rolled oats. Stir flour, baking powder and baking soda together and add. Mix. Roll into 1 inch balls. Place on greased baking sheet. Flatten with fork. If fork sticks, dip in flour. Bake in 375°F oven for 8 to 10 minutes until lightly browned. Makes about 6 dozen.

Pictured on page 71.

# Turtle Cookies

*Snappy and cute. A birthday party special.*

| | |
|---|---|
| Butter (or hard margarine), softened | 1/2 cup |
| Brown sugar, packed | 1/2 cup |
| Large egg | 1 |
| Egg yolk (large) | 1 |
| Vanilla | 1/4 tsp. |
| Maple flavoring | 1/8 tsp. |
| All-purpose flour | 1 1/2 cups |
| Baking soda | 1/4 tsp. |
| Salt | 1/4 tsp. |

*(continued on next page)*

| Pecan halves, split | 1 1/2 cups |
| Egg white (large), fork beaten | 1 |

Semisweet chocolate chips

Cream butter and sugar together. Beat in egg, yolk and flavorings.

Stir in flour, baking soda and salt. Shape into 1 inch balls.

Place 3 nut pieces on greased cookie sheet to form head and 2 front legs plus 2 pieces for back legs. Dip bottom of ball into egg white. Place in center of shaped nuts. Flatten slightly. Bake in 350°F oven for 10 to 12 minutes.

Place 6 to 8 semisweet chocolate chips on each hot cookie. Allow them to melt, then spread with knife. Chocolate icing may be used as an alternative. Makes 3 1/2 dozen.

Pictured on page 35.

# Cherry Winks

*A combination of cereal, fruit and nuts produces a pretty party cookie.*

| Butter (or hard margarine), softened | 3/4 cup |
| Granulated sugar | 1 cup |
| Large eggs | 2 |
| All-purpose flour | 2 cups |
| Baking powder | 1 tsp. |
| Baking soda | 1/2 tsp. |
| Salt | 1/2 tsp. |
| Chopped pecans or walnuts | 1 cup |
| Chopped dates or raisins | 1 cup |
| Cornflakes or other cereal flakes | 3 cups |
| Maraschino cherries, halved or quartered, blotted dry | 15–30 |

Cream butter and sugar together in bowl. Beat in eggs.

Stir flour, baking powder, baking soda and salt together and add along with nuts and dates. Mix well. Shape into small balls.

Crush cornflakes into crumbs. Roll balls in crumbs. Place on greased baking sheet. Top with half or quarter cherry. Bake in 350°F oven for 10 to 12 minutes. Makes 4 to 5 dozen.

Pictured on page 17.

# Fattigman

*A Scandinavian Christmas cookie that is deep-fried. It makes a*
*large batch that keeps for months in the freezer.*

| | |
|---|---|
| Whipping cream | 1/2 cup |
| Large eggs | 2 |
| Egg yolks (large) | 3 |
| Granulated sugar | 1/2 cup |
| Butter (or hard margarine), softened | 1/4 cup |
| Brandy (or use 1 1/2 tsp. brandy flavoring plus water) | 3 tbsp. |
| Cardamom | 1/2 tsp. |
| All-purpose flour | 2 1/2 cups |

Fat for deep-frying
Icing (confectioner's) sugar for dusting

In small bowl beat cream until stiff. Set aside.

Using same beaters beat eggs and yolks in large mixing bowl until frothy.
Add sugar and beat well. Beat in butter. Add brandy, cardamom and
whipping cream. Stir.

Add flour. Stir. Let batter stand in refrigerator overnight. Next day roll
thinly. Cut into diamond shapes 2 × 5 inches. Cut slit in center. Pull 1 end
through slit or leave flat.

Deep-fry a few at a time in hot fat 375°F. Drain on paper towel. These are
sweet enough to serve plain. Dust with icing sugar if desired. Makes about
8 dozen.

Pictured on page 17.

### Paré Pointer
*A common greeting from the rake in the garden — "Hi, hoe!"*

# Peanut Oatmeal Cookies

*Chewy peanut butter flavored treats for everyone.*

| | |
|---|---|
| Butter (or hard margarine), softened | 1/2 cup |
| Brown sugar, packed | 1 cup |
| Large egg | 1 |
| Vanilla | 1/2 tsp. |
| Smooth peanut butter | 1/2 cup |
| Rolled oats | 2 cups |
| Whole wheat flour (or all-purpose) | 1/2 cup |
| Baking powder | 1/2 tsp. |
| Baking soda | 1/2 tsp. |
| Salt | 1/4 tsp. |

Cream butter and sugar together. Beat in egg. Add vanilla and peanut butter.

Mix in remaining ingredients. Shape into small balls or drop by spoonfuls onto ungreased cookie sheet allowing room for expansion. Bake in 375°F oven for 12 to 15 minutes. Makes about 3 dozen.

Pictured on page 53.

# Hedge Hogs

*Soft and chewy. A snap to make.*

| | |
|---|---|
| Butter (or hard margarine), melted | 2 tbsp. |
| Brown sugar, packed | 1 cup |
| Chopped walnuts | 2 cups |
| Chopped dates | 2 cups |
| All-purpose flour | 1/2 cup |
| Vanilla | 2 tsp. |
| Large eggs | 2 |
| Coconut, shredded or medium | |

Measure first 7 ingredients into bowl. Mix together well. Shape into small balls.

Roll balls in coconut. Place on greased baking sheet. Bake in 350°F oven for 10 to 12 minutes. Makes about 3 1/2 dozen.

Pictured on page 35.

# Chinese Almond Cookies

*To obtain the true flavor for these cookies, lard is required.*

| | |
|---|---|
| Lard, room temperature | 1 cup |
| Granulated sugar | 1 cup |
| Large egg | 1 |
| Almond flavoring | 2 tsp. |
| All-purpose flour | 2 1/2 cups |
| Baking powder | 1 tsp. |
| Salt | 1 tsp. |
| Blanched almonds | 48 |
| Large egg | 1 |
| Water | 1 tbsp. |

In mixing bowl, cream lard and sugar. Beat in 1 egg and almond flavoring.

Stir flour, baking powder and salt together and add. Mix. Roll into 48 balls. Arrange on lightly greased baking sheets.

Place whole almond in center. Press with glass to flatten ball somewhat. Beat 1 egg with water. Brush egg and water mixture over cookies. Bake in 350°F oven for 8 to 12 minutes until lightly browned. Makes 4 dozen.

Pictured on page 53.

# Lemon Cracks

*These golden cookies have real lemon flavor. Refreshing.*

| | |
|---|---|
| Butter (or hard margarine), softened | 1/2 cup |
| Granulated sugar | 1/4 cup |
| Brown sugar, packed | 1/2 cup |
| Large egg | 1 |
| Grated lemon rind | 1 tbsp. |
| Lemon juice | 2 tbsp. |
| All-purpose flour | 1 1/2 cups |
| Baking powder | 1 tsp. |
| Baking soda | 1/2 tsp. |
| Granulated sugar | |

(continued on next page)

Cream butter and next 2 sugars. Beat in egg. Add lemon rind and juice.

Stir flour, baking powder and baking soda together and add. Mix well. Shape into balls.

Roll in sugar. Place on ungreased sheet. Bake in 350°F oven for 10 to 15 minutes. Makes 4 dozen.

**Variation:** Add 2 cups raisins.

Pictured on page 53.

---

# Cookie Caps

*These are topped with meringue before baking.*
*They freeze well. A different cookie.*

| | |
|---|---|
| Butter (or hard margarine), softened | 1/2 cup |
| Granulated sugar | 1/2 cup |
| Large egg | 1 |
| Milk | 2 tbsp. |
| All-purpose flour | 1 1/2 cups |
| Baking powder | 1/2 tsp. |
| MERINGUE TOPPING | |
| Egg white (large), room temperature | 1 |
| Cream of tartar | 1/8 tsp. |
| Brown or granulated sugar | 2 tbsp. |
| Vanilla | 1/2 tsp. |
| Semisweet chocolate chips | 1/2 cup |

Cream butter and sugar. Beat in egg and milk.

Add flour and baking powder. Stir. Shape into small balls. Place on ungreased pan. Flatten with sugared glass.

**Meringue Topping:** Beat egg white and cream of tartar until soft peaks form. Add sugar in 2 additions beating until stiff. Fold in vanilla and chips. Put a dab on top of each cookie. Bake in 325°F oven for 15 to 20 minutes. Makes about 3 dozen.

Pictured on page 125.

# Peanut Blossoms

*These really do look like blossoms.*

| | |
|---|---|
| All-purpose flour | 1 3/4 cups |
| Granulated sugar | 1/2 cup |
| Brown sugar, packed | 1/2 cup |
| Baking soda | 1 tsp. |
| Salt | 1/2 tsp. |
| Large egg | 1 |
| Butter (or hard margarine), softened | 1/2 cup |
| Smooth peanut butter | 1/2 cup |
| Milk | 2 tbsp. |
| Vanilla | 1 tsp. |
| Granulated sugar | 1/3 cup |
| Chocolate buds or kisses | 72 |

Measure first 10 ingredients into mixing bowl. Beat on low speed until a dough forms. Shape into small 1 inch balls.

Roll in sugar and place on ungreased cookie sheet. Do not press down. Bake in 375°F oven for 10 to 12 minutes.

Top with a chocolate kiss immediately. Press down until cookie cracks around the edges. Makes about 6 dozen.

Pictured on page 53.

---

### Paré Pointer
*The man who supplies a pickle factory*
*with cucumbers is the farmer in the dill.*

# Peanut Butter Cookies

*Makes a huge batch but can easily be halved. Certain children have been raised on these. A family favorite. One serving is as many as can be held between thumb and index finger.*

| | |
|---|---|
| Butter (or hard margarine), softened | 1 cup |
| Brown sugar, packed | 1 cup |
| Granulated sugar | 1 cup |
| Large eggs | 2 |
| Smooth peanut butter | 1 cup |
| All-purpose flour | 3 cups |
| Baking soda | 2 tsp. |
| Salt | 1/4 tsp. |

Cream butter and both sugars together. Beat in eggs, 1 at a time. Mix in peanut butter.

Stir in flour, baking soda and salt. Shape into small balls. Place on ungreased cookie sheets allowing room for expansion. Press with fork. Dip fork in flour as needed to prevent batter stickiness. Bake in 375°F oven for 12 to 15 minutes. Makes 6 dozen.

**PEANUT BUTTER CHIP COOKIES:** Add 1 to 2 cups semisweet chocolate chips.

**PEANUT BUTTER JELLY NESTS:** Shape dough into 1 inch balls. Place on cookie sheet. Press with thumb to indent. Bake in 375°F oven for 5 minutes. Press again. Bake for 7 to 10 minutes more. Fill with red raspberry or strawberry jelly while cookies are still warm or store and fill as needed.

Pictured on cover.

**LOLLIPOPS:** To make peanut butter lollipops see method for Rolled Ginger Cookies on page 93.

### Paré Pointer
*Of course a sneeze is usually pointed Atchoo!*

# Lemon Pie Cookies

*A crisp cookie just right for dunking. A lemon pie filling is used for these.*

| | |
|---|---|
| Butter (or hard margarine), softened | 1 cup |
| Brown sugar, packed | 1/2 cup |
| Lemon pudding and pie filling mix,<br>  1 pie size, not instant | 1 |
| Water | 1 tbsp. |
| | |
| All-purpose flour | 2 cups |
| Chopped walnuts | 1/2 cup |

Cream butter and sugar together. Mix in dry pie filling and water.

Add flour and nuts. Mix well. Shape into 1 inch balls. Place on ungreased baking sheet. Leave some as is. Press others with fork. Bake in 325°F oven for 12 to 15 minutes until golden. While hot, dip into Lemon Dip. Makes about 5 dozen.

**LEMON DIP:** Put 3 tbsp. lemon juice and 1/4 cup granulated sugar into small saucepan. Heat and stir to dissolve. Dip cookie tops. Let stand to dry.

Pictured on page 53.

# Coco Rum Diagonals

*Coconut flavored cookies topped with rum icing.*

| | |
|---|---|
| Butter (or hard margarine), softened | 1/2 cup |
| Granulated sugar | 1/4 cup |
| Vanilla | 1 tsp. |
| Salt | 1/8 tsp. |
| | |
| All-purpose flour | 1 cup |
| Baking powder | 1/2 tsp. |
| Flaked coconut | 1 cup |

ICING
| | |
|---|---|
| Icing (confectioner's) sugar | 1 cup |
| Water | 1 1/2 tbsp. |
| Rum flavoring | 1/2 tsp. |

(continued on next page)

Measure first 4 ingredients into bowl. Beat until fluffy.

Stir flour and baking powder together. Add along with coconut. Mix. Make 6 ropes, 9 inches long. Place on greased baking sheet. Bake in 350°F oven for 18 to 20 minutes. Ice while warm.

**Icing:** Mix all 3 ingredients together. Add more water or icing sugar to make proper spreading consistency. Ice strips while slightly warm. Cut into 1 inch diagonals.

Pictured on page 125.

# Cherry Surprise

*These chocolate covered cherries are a popular flavor combination.*

| | |
|---|---|
| Butter (or hard margarine), softened | 1/2 cup |
| Granulated sugar | 1 cup |
| Cocoa, sifted | 1/4 cup |
| Large egg | 1 |
| All-purpose flour | 1 cup |
| Salt | 1/8 tsp. |
| Chopped walnuts | 1/2 cup |
| Maraschino cherries, well drained | 48 |

In mixing bowl, cream butter and sugar together with spoon. Stir in cocoa. Add egg and beat with spoon.

Stir in flour, salt and nuts. Chill for 30 minutes.

Blot cherries dry with paper towels. Pinch off small piece of dough. Flatten with fingers and wrap around cherry to enclose completely. Place on ungreased cookie sheet. Bake in 375°F oven for 10 to 12 minutes. Glaze. Makes 4 dozen.

**GLAZE:** Stir enough maraschino cherry juice into 1 cup icing (confectioner's) sugar to make a barely pourable glaze. Dip cookies or spoon over top. Allow to dry.

**CHOCOLATE MINT SURPRISE:** Wrap dough around solid chocolate wafer that has a mint flavor.

Pictured on page 35.

# Sesame Snackers

*Excellent nutty flavor to these.*

| | |
|---|---|
| Cooking oil | 3/4 cup |
| Brown sugar, packed | 1 1/2 cups |
| Large egg | 1 |
| Vanilla | 1 tsp. |
| | |
| All-purpose flour | 2 cups |
| Baking powder | 1 tsp. |
| Salt | 1/4 tsp. |
| Sesame seeds, toasted in 350°F oven for 10 to 15 minutes to brown, stirring twice | 1/2 cup |

Toasted sesame seeds for topping

Combine cooking oil, sugar, egg and vanilla in mixing bowl. Beat well.

Add flour, baking powder, salt and first amount of sesame seeds. Stir well. Shape into small balls. Place on ungreased baking sheet. Flatten with glass.

Sprinkle with sesame seeds. Bake in 350°F oven for 8 to 10 minutes. Makes 4 dozen.

Pictured on page 89.

# Snickerdoodles

*The aroma of these baking will bring everyone to the kitchen for some samples.*

| | |
|---|---|
| Butter (or hard margarine), softened | 1 cup |
| Granulated sugar | 1 1/2 cups |
| Large eggs | 2 |
| All-purpose flour (see note) | 2 1/2 cups |
| Cream of tartar | 2 tsp. |
| Baking soda | 1 tsp. |
| Salt | 1/4 tsp. |
| Granulated sugar | 2 tbsp. |
| Cinnamon | 2 tsp. |

Cream butter and first amount of sugar well. Beat in eggs 1 at a time.

Mix in flour, cream of tartar, baking soda and salt. Shape into 1 inch balls.

Stir remaining sugar and cinnamon together in small dish. Roll balls in mixture to coat. Place on ungreased cookie sheet. Bake in 400°F oven for 7 to 8 minutes. Makes about 4 dozen.

Pictured on page 35.

**Note:** If cookie dough is too sticky, up to 1/4 cup flour may be added.

---

### Paré Pointer

*Johnny fed the cat pennies when his mother told him to put something in the kitty.*

# Rosettes

*A crisp deep-fried Scandinavian cookie that is not too sweet.*
*Made with a rosette iron.*

| | |
|---|---|
| Large eggs | 2 |
| Granulated sugar | 1 tbsp. |
| Milk | 1 cup |
| All-purpose flour | 1 cup |
| Salt | 1/2 tsp. |

Fat for deep-frying

Beat eggs with a spoon in mixing bowl. Add sugar and milk. Stir in flour and salt mixing until smooth.

Heat rosette iron in hot fat 375°F for about 1 minute. Dip into batter almost to the top (not over) of the mold. Immerse in hot fat completely covering mold. Fry until golden, about 25 to 35 seconds. Bubbles almost will have stopped. Gently push cookie off rosette. Place upside down on waxed paper to drain. May be frozen at this point. To serve, sprinkle with icing (confectioner's) sugar. Makes 3 to 3 1/2 dozen.

Pictured on page 143.

# Melting Moments

*These small delicate cookies are attractive when sandwiched with tinted icing.*
*A cherry turns a "drop" into a festive treat.*

| | |
|---|---|
| Butter (not margarine), softened | 1 cup |
| Icing (confectioner's) sugar | 1/3 cup |
| Vanilla | 1 tsp. |
| All-purpose flour | 1 1/2 cups |
| Cornstarch | 1/2 cup |

Mix together well. Knead to form ball of dough. Pinch off small pieces of dough. Place on ungreased cookie sheet. If you prefer, roll into 1 inch balls. Press with fork or glass. Bake in 325°F oven for 12 to 15 minutes. Sandwich together with colored icing or serve plain. Makes 5 dozen.

**Variation:** Drop by spoonfuls onto baking sheet. Press cherry or pecan halves into centers.

Pictured on page 17.

**...es**

*...d nut center.*

| | |
|---|---|
| | 1 cup |
| | 1 cup |
| | 2 tsp. |
| | 1/2 cup |
| | 1/2 cup |
| | 2 |
| | 2 cups |
| | 1 tsp. |

...rocessor. Mix with lemon juice. Form into marble-size balls, ...

Cream butter and sugar together. Add beaten eggs.

Stir flour and baking powder together and add. Mix well. Roll into 60 small balls. Flatten each and wrap around marble balls. Place on ungreased baking sheet.

Sprinkle (or dip) tops with granulated sugar. Bake in 350°F oven until light brown, about 15 minutes. Makes 5 dozen.

Pictured on page 35.

---

### Paré Pointer

*Cross a parrot and a woodpecker and you will get a
bird that talks in Morse code.*

# Swedish Tea Cakes

*You will need to double this recipe. Also known as*
*Swedish Pastry and Thumbprints.*

| | |
|---|---|
| Butter (or hard margarine), softened | 1/2 cup |
| Brown sugar, packed | 1/4 cup |
| Egg yolk (large) | 1 |
| All-purpose flour | 1 cup |
| Baking powder | 1/2 tsp. |
| Salt | 1/8 tsp. |
| Egg white (large), fork beaten | 1 |
| Finely chopped nuts for coating | 2/3 cup |
| Jam or jelly (red is best) | |

Cream butter and sugar together. Beat in egg yolk.

Stir flour, baking powder and salt together and add. Mix. Shape into small balls.

Dip into egg white, roll in nuts and place on greased baking sheet. Dent each with your thumb. Bake in 325°F oven for 5 minutes. Remove and press dents again. Continue to bake for 10 to 15 minutes until golden brown.

Fill dents with jam while warm, or store unfilled to be filled as used. Makes about 20.

Pictured on page 17.

---

## Paré Pointer

*When bankers dance, they do the vaults.*

# Palmiers

*These brown caramelized cookies add to any tray of goodies.*
*Sometimes known as Palm Leaves, this is puff pastry at its best.*

Frozen puff pastry, thawed                                    14 oz.

Icing (confectioner's) sugar or granulated

Generously sprinkle counter with sugar. Roll half of the pastry at a time to a long rectangle 6 × 12 inches in size. Using a pastry brush dipped in water moisten the surface very slightly. Roll each long side to meet in center. Press rolls together lightly. Wrap in plastic or waxed paper and chill thoroughly.

To bake, cut into slices 1/4 inch thick. Dip cut sides into sugar on counter. Place on greased baking sheet allowing room for expansion. Bake in 400°F oven for about 10 minutes until a rich caramelized brown. These must be turned over halfway through baking to brown evenly on both sides. Makes 5 dozen.

**PUFF BALLS:** Roll pastry 1/4 inch thick. Cut into 2 inch rounds. Dip in granulated sugar and place on greased baking sheet. These must be turned over halfway through baking. Bake in 375°F oven for about 10 minutes. Makes 5 dozen.

Pictured on page 53.

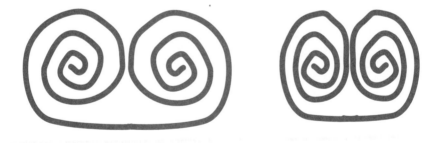

# Guide to Reading the Recipes

## Ingredient Definitions

Here are the answers to some of your most frequently asked ingredient questions.

| | |
|---|---|
| **Dessert topping** | Whipped topping (in a powder), such as Dream Whip™ |
| **English cucumber** | Thin-skinned, seedless cucumber often sold individually shrinkwrapped in plastic |
| **Fancy molasses** | Lighter-colored molasses commonly used in baking — not blackstrap, which has a stronger flavor |
| **Hard margarine** | Stick margarine – 1/2 cup equals 1 stick |
| **Icing (confectioner's) sugar** | Powdered sugar |
| **Salad dressing** | Spoonable type of dressing, such as Miracle Whip™ |

## Measurement Equivalents

Package and can sizes may vary across the country. The chart below will help you determine the right amount of each ingredient.

| | | |
|---|---|---|
| 3 tsp. | 1 tbsp. | 1/2 fluid ounce |
| 2 tbsp. | 1/8 cup | 1 fluid ounce |
| 4 tbsp. | 1/4 cup | 2 fluid ounces |
| 8 tbsp. | 1/2 cup | 4 fluid ounces |
| 12 tbsp. | 3/4 cup | 6 fluid ounces |
| 16 tbsp. | 1 cup | 8 fluid ounces |
| 32 tbsp. | 2 cups | 16 fluid ounces |
| 64 tbsp. | 4 cups | 32 fluid ounces |

Choosing a casserole dish? These cup equivalents will help with the task.

| | |
|---|---|
| 1 quart | 4 cups |
| 1 1/2 quarts | 6 cups |
| 2 quarts | 8 cups |
| 2 1/2 quarts | 10 cups |
| 3 quarts | 12 cups |
| 4 quarts | 16 cups |
| 5 quarts | 20 cups |

# Recipe Index

**152**

**153**

**155**

# Notes

# Notes

# Notes

# Company's Coming Cookbook Series

| Title: | Price | Quantity | Total |
|---|---|---|---|
| Chicken, Etc. | $12.99 | | |
| Cook For Kids | $12.99 | | |
| Cookies | $12.99 | | |
| Garden Greens | $12.99 | | |
| Low-Fat Cooking | $12.99 | | |
| Recipes For Leftovers | $12.99 | | |
| Rush-Hour Recipes | $12.99 | | |
| Slow Cooker Recipes | $12.99 | | |
| Starters | $12.99 | | |
| Stir-Fry | $12.99 | | |
| Sweet Cravings | $12.99 | | |
| The Beef Book | $12.99 | | |
| The Egg Book | $12.99 | | |
| The Rookie Cook | $12.99 | | |
| Year-Round Grilling | $12.99 | | |
| FL Residents ONLY Please Include Local Sales Tax | | | |
| TOTALS | | | |
| **TOTAL AMOUNT DUE** | | | |

## SHIP TO:

Name:_____

Address:_____

_____

_____

City:_____ State:_____ Zip Code:_____

Phone # (include area code):_____

Name of store where purchased:_____

**Please make Check or Money Order payable and mail to:**
Company's Coming USA, L.C.
1060 Maitland Center Commons, Suite 365
Maitland, FL 32751

**Please Allow 4 to 6 Weeks for Delivery**